SUPERBOLD

FROM UNDER-CONFIDENT TO CHARISMATIC IN 90 DAYS

FRED JOYAL

SUPERBOLD

From Under-Confident to Charismatic in 90 Days

ISBN 978-1-5445-2307-1 *Hardcover*
       978-1-5445-2306-4 *Ebook*
       978-1-5445-2308-8 *Audiobook*

To

Robert King Dee,

as great a friend and

mentor as I could ever

have wished for.

TABLE OF CONTENTS

PART IV—THE BOLDNESS EXERCISES

PART V—SUPERBOLDNESS

INTRODUCTION

Boldness is a superpower.

What do I mean by that? I mean, compared to average human beings, bold individuals seize life in remarkable, almost unbelievable ways. They run for president. They succeed in business, in careers, in love, and they generally have a really good time. Bold people walk up to supermodels and ask them to dance. They stand in front of audiences and tell jokes, not even minding when people don't laugh. They sing karaoke—badly—sober. Every weekend. They divorce an unsuitable husband even though their culture forbids it. They sit at the front of the room and ask questions. They start companies. They climb under the velvet ropes to meet a rock star or sneak into a nightclub. Or maybe they refuse to move to the back of the bus, like Rosa Parks. Or they're a politician who decides he can end slavery or the Cold War.

Most of all, they don't miss out on opportunities, and so they don't have a head full of regrets.

Boldness is a gift, but it's not something you're gifted with or born with. It's a gift you give yourself. In other words, boldness is not innate. That's right. It's not a genetic limitation. It's not a mutation a chosen few are born with. Boldness can be learned. You can develop it. Refine it. Expand it to whatever level you choose. Harness it for your own good, and perhaps the good of the world.

I know, because I learned it. I taught myself to become bolder, and I can teach you.

I see boldness as something even greater than self-confidence. Because bold people aren't just confident. They actively pursue things, attempt things, and achieve things that even confident people don't. Boldness is self-confidence in action.

Bold people also get away with things that most people wouldn't dare to attempt. I'm not talking about committing crimes here (although it takes quite a bit of boldness to be a cat burglar!). I'm talking about work situations, play situations, random encounters, and fleeting opportunities that bold people will leap at without a moment's hesitation. They get further, they experience more joy, they pursue their dreams with passion and determination, and when they encounter an obstacle, they leap over, or tunnel under, or power straight through. They don't hesitate.

That's a word that will come up in this book over and over: hesitation. How often have you hesitated, when in retrospect you should have acted? If you're like most people, and especially if you're under-confident, the list is long. How many times in your life have you missed a great opportunity, a chance to change the course of your life, because you didn't speak up? How many sales have you missed? How many promotions? How many relationships? How many unique moments? How many adventures? How much fun?

But what if you never missed an opportunity again? What if you never had a regret about something you could have done or should have done? How much better would your life be?

I'm guessing quite a bit.

As you develop your boldness to others, you will appear charismatic. They will believe you were always that way. But your charisma, which is what you will have, is simply your boldness emanating from you like a positive energy field.

This book is about bringing boldness into your daily life, making it your new default behavior, so you realize the amazing power it gives you, and that it allows you to chase your dreams. More than that, it will give you the stairway to your dreams. Because a dream without a plan is just a daydream. And that plan requires action. Bold action.

WHO IS THIS BOOK FOR?

Are you shy or bold? Most people would say they are somewhere in-between. But the fact is, in any given situation, you act either shy or bold. There is no in-between. You either spoke up or you didn't. You either hesitated or you didn't. You either acted or you didn't. There is no middle ground. It doesn't matter if you *almost* spoke up. You still acted either without confidence (shy) or with confidence (bold).

So which one are you?

Here's the main problem: for most people, their response is not in their control. The *situation* determines whether they can summon boldness or not. So they miss great opportunities, they have tremendous regrets and, conversely, when they do act boldly, they can't figure out how to do it consistently, especially when it would matter the most.

Have you ever walked into a party where you didn't know anyone and then left an hour later without talking to a single person? I have.

Have you ever missed the opportunity to tell someone how interested you were in them? I have.

Have you ever see a famous person, or someone you really admired, and not gone up and talked to them?

Have you ever not asked for something that you really wanted, like a promotion, and then seen someone else ask and get it?

Have you ever avoided doing something that would have been fun, exciting, or satisfying, because you were afraid you might embarrass yourself?

Let me tell you how often I've done all these things: so often I've lost track.

So let me do this backward. I'll describe the person who doesn't need this book, and you decide what's true for you.

- If you are confident in every situation and can walk up to any stranger and start a conversation, no matter if it's a homeless person or the British prime minister or Beyoncé;
- If you don't hesitate for a single second when you see a unique opportunity to participate;
- If you never feel embarrassed drawing attention to yourself;
- If you can ask for the order in every sales pitch;
- If you can comfortably give a person strong criticism and have them still like you;
- If you have the life partner you want;
- If your work is satisfying, and you feel you are advancing in your career as fast as you want;
- If you believe you can communicate your thoughts effectively in any situation;
- If you have zero stage fright;
- If your social circle is as wide and deep as you want it to be.

If all of these are true, then you can stop reading. You don't need this book. However, if some—or perhaps all—of these things are *not* true for you, then the techniques in this book can take you as far into boldness as you want to go, all the way to superbold. From wherever you are right now, I can help you get to a place unimaginable to your current self.

The first step is acknowledging you want change. I sincerely believe people who experience shyness don't want to. But they often define themselves with that word, and that's the first belief I'm going to attack. You are not shy. You *feel* shy. Sometimes. Sometimes you behave in a way that is inhibited, reticent, withdrawn, under-confident. That is not *what* you are, and it is certainly not *who* you are. You may be short or tall, Black or Hispanic, myopic or bowlegged. You *are* those things. But shyness—and any level of under-confidence—is simply a conditioned behavior that you exhibit. Shyness is not a genetic disorder.

Not that it isn't part of who you are right now. It is. For some of you, a lack of confidence may be the biggest part of your personality. But it's not permanent. I guarantee it. You know how I know? Because I'll bet there are dozens of situations where you don't feel hesitant or under-confident at all. Maybe it's with close friends, or with family, or even at work. As I said, it's *situational*. But, unfortunately, those situations are often the most important ones. It's not you, not all the time, but it is how you behave sometimes. Which means it can change.

Here is a good reason to cultivate your boldness. You are not just depriving yourself of experiences—friendships, job opportunities, relationships, camaraderie—but you are depriving *others* of the experience of *you*. You have something to offer the world. There are people out there who would love to know you, but they may never meet you because you are hiding in your cave. You may even have something significant to offer to the world at large, and a lack of boldness is keeping you from achieving your destiny. Perhaps you would be a phenomenal senator, or an exceptional entrepreneur. Or a breakthrough comedienne. Who's to say?

The ultimate goal of this book is superboldness. What I mean by that is you are bold on command, all the time, anytime, in any situation. It is never restricted by the circumstances or the magnitude of the challenge. It is a superpower you summon as naturally as breathing.

I'm going to get you to this place where you will feel charismatic. And I'm going to do it so fast you'll be rather shocked. I did it the hard, slow way, over decades. But I figured out a systematic way to bring out my boldness in any situation that I chose. And it has changed my life. I'm different than people who are bold but don't know why or how they are, because I had to learn how to be bold. I have a system that worked for me so well that I am superbold because it is part of me, my true natural essence. And you can learn it too.

Are you ready to start chasing your dreams? It's a lifelong journey. But it starts by acknowledging that who you are right now is not who you want to be. Then I can show you how to quickly and effectively change all those things you want to change. Just as I've done for myself.

This book is about discovering who you might become, if you only dared.

PART I

BOLDNESS DECODED

CHAPTER 1

WHY BOLDNESS?

"When I let go of who I am, I discover who I might become."
—Lao Tzu

If you ask people who know me now, they will tell you I am gregarious, outgoing, bold, daring, and an extrovert. Some have even called me charismatic. I say this not to brag, but because if you ask someone who knew me in my youth if I was *any* of those things, they would find your question hilarious. "Fred?" they would say. "You've got to be kidding. You've clearly never met the guy."

The fact is, I grew up extremely shy. Because of that, I have several big regrets and countless small ones. I blew my first real job promotion because I couldn't pick up the phone and make even a single cold call. I spent two days with Robin Williams and never told him that he starred in two of my favorite movies, *Good Will Hunting* and *Dead Poets Society*. I never eulogized my father, and it is one of the greatest regrets of my life not to have spoken and honored the man who raised me, taught me to be a man, made countless sacrifices along the way, and died too young. For things like this, there are no second chances.

That's not me anymore. I realized that the few times I *did* speak up, that I did suppress my shyness and act boldly, were the times that made all the difference in my life.

Let me give you a simple example.

I was fourteen, hanging around the local boys' club, waiting for my turn to shoot pool, when an older man came bursting through the door. He was looking for one of the other boys, who was not there at the time. The man was agitated. "He's supposed to be washing dishes for me tonight," he said, frustrated.

From the corner of the room, a meek little voice said, "I'll work."

The man jerked his head toward me. "Who said that?" he shouted.

"Me," I replied.

"Come with me!" he commanded.

I followed him as he rushed out of the club and jumped into his Cadillac El Dorado convertible, and we sped off to his restaurant, where I worked a ten-hour shift for a dollar an hour. Cash.

Let me tell you all that came from that moment where I decided to speak up.

That dishwashing job turned into a cooking job, and then bartending, which I used to support myself all through college.

Gary, the owner's son, has become one of my oldest and dearest friends, and eventually a partner in my business as well.

Recently, as an "uncle" to Gary's two sons, I am their partner in another very successful business functioning as an advisor, investor, and friend to these two boys I have come to love almost like sons.

But the friendship with Gary by itself would have been reward enough.

I could have sat there in that boys' club and said nothing, and that friendship and that pathway that had so many benefits in my life would never have begun. It was not until many years later that I connected that briefest moment of daring—which, for someone as shy as I was, was extremely rare—with the power of boldness. I learned from it. I learned how to summon it to create many of those powerful chain reactions. And I've learned to trust that I won't be able to necessarily see all the potential rewards that may come to me. But I now know that they will undoubtedly come and enrich my life even more than I anticipated.

That's what I want for you. It's why I wrote this book.

WHY DEVELOP BOLDNESS?

Everything Flows from It

My friend Will has a six-year-old boy, and whenever his son is hesitant, shy, or worried about what other kids might think, Will tells him this: "Boldness is a superpower." Will heard this from me in a lecture a few years ago, and not only has he never forgotten it, he drills it into his son's consciousness so that he never misses out on anything in life.

I love that Will does this. Because if someone asked me, "If you could give your child only one thing, what would it be?" my answer would be "boldness." Because everything flows from that. Anything is possible when you are acting with self-confidence. Don't believe me? Imagine what level of self-confidence it takes to run for president. Yet any US citizen over thirty-five can choose to run. All you have to do is say, "I'm running for president," professing your desire to be the leader of the free world, and you're on the path to what's possible. One sentence.

But it doesn't start without boldness.

Trust me, I know. I didn't develop confidence growing up. I was a nerdy kid with glasses who skipped the second grade, so I was always smaller and younger than my classmates. And so, I became painfully shy. I let it define me. Until I got so angry at how much I was missing out on that I figured out how to redefine myself. I met bold people, and I marveled at their behavior, at how much they didn't care what people thought. They just lived wonderful lives. Then I used every resource I could to transform myself.

Now I get excited at the idea of getting up in front of two thousand people. I walk into a huge empty conference hall and think, "I would love to be in front of a crowd in this room."

It's not about the glory and attention of being in front of an audience. In fact, some of those people will think I'm an idiot/bore/attention whore. I guarantee it. But a few of them will have a moment of epiphany, where they will hear me say something, hear an example I give or an analogy, or just the right turn of a phrase that clicks with them, and suddenly they have an insight about their lives, their business, their mistakes. Or I may just make them laugh.

I sincerely believe that your under-confidence, your hesitance to interact with other people, is diminishing you. It is closing in the light of your personality, your uniqueness, and depriving others of who you really are.

With my boldness, I create change. My actions, simple as they may be, ripple out into the world and have an impact. You know those people you've been labeling as "charismatic"? It's their boldness. It's coming off them in waves, and they're moving through the world with it, making the changes they want. Many people—and I know this because they've told me—perceive me as charismatic for precisely this reason.

Cultivate your boldness. Everything flows from it.

You've Paid the Price for Hesitation

One of the biggest reasons to develop your boldness is because you've already paid the price for your *unboldness*.

I'm going to use two words a lot in this book, so I want to be clear about their definitions. The first word is *hesitant*, which most people understand, and it applies broadly to all types of actions, from speaking to dancing to diving off a ten-meter platform. The second word is *reticent*, which means "hesitant to speak." Often you will hear people misuse the word *reticent* to mean *hesitant*, or they will say, "I'm reticent to speak," which is essentially saying it twice. What they mean is "reluctant to speak."

Suffice it to say that I will be using these words in their actual meanings. I'll be using them a lot because the hallmark of under-confidence is hesitation, in words or in actions.

Hesitation haunts us. Sometimes the opportunity passes in just a few seconds, but other times we'll burn up five or ten minutes, or longer, letting that attractive woman or man stand alone in the corner and, just as we summon the nerve to vocalize something, someone else walks up to them.

Or the right moment to ask for a promotion passes because the other person at your level asked first and got it.

Or you see a famous person you want to talk to. Or you have a great idea in a business meeting but are waiting to be asked what you think.

Or worse, when you wanted to speak up about some injustice or offensive behavior and didn't. I'm sure you can recall dozens of times when that happened.

We let chances slip away, and we've done it so often, we think it's normal. It's not. But, just as it would not be normal to fly to Hong Kong and suddenly be able to speak Cantonese, we shouldn't expect to instantly change just because we don't want to be hesitant anymore. It takes practice.

Undoubtedly, you've experienced more than once how hesitation is not rewarded. You've watched that window of opportunity close as you overponder a situation and play out scenarios in your head. So, let me help you with these painful memories. It's not really because you're shy or lack confidence. It's because you're not prepared. You haven't developed the right skills yet.

In other words, it's nothing to beat yourself up about, just something to fix.

This book will help you. At the end of this chapter, I'll give you a road map of how you're going to move past your under-confidence and be bolder, until people you meet will think you were always this charismatic.

But for now, my hope is that you are at a place where you don't want to be defined by your lack of confidence, your lack of boldness, and are ready to learn how to transform yourself.

Because life is too short.

It's too short to let other people decide what you're capable of.

It's too short to sit waiting for your dreams to come true.

It's too short to spend time waiting for the perfect mate to come along.

It's too short to think other people care if you blame them for your unhappiness.

It's too short to put off taking responsibility for everything that is important in your life.

It's too short to be lonely one more second, to not be alone except when you choose to be.

It's too short not to laugh more than you complain, smile more than you frown, and win more than you lose.

It's too short to spend it avoiding all risk.

It's too short to spend it avoiding all pain.

It's too short to spend your time judging other people.

It's too short to avoid chasing your dreams with determination, persistence, and a little madness.

So look before you leap. But, no matter what, leap.

You Will Always Be Ready

The biggest WHY in terms of developing your boldness is not the day-to-day impact on your life which, don't get me wrong, I consider very important. The real WHY is because you never know when that moment is going to come, that moment when you are going to need this skill for what may become one of the most important days or events or encounters in your life. You don't know if that will occur tomorrow or next month, or ten years from now. But you'll want to be up to the task.

I'll say it again: one of the most important reasons to master this skill is because there will be singular moments, opportunities to speak or act that will occur only once in your life, and you'll want to be ready. That's where superboldness comes in. You will always be ready.

You know the expression, "No one died wishing they spent more time at the office." This will be true for you with respect to your boldness. You will not regret your boldest moves, but rather your most cautious ones, your most hesitant ones, your words unspoken, your risks not taken. My goal is to make your final words be, "I changed myself constantly, took incredible chances, and found love, joy, and adventure in abundance. I died bruised, broken, worn out, fully depleted in every way, with a big, satisfied smile on my face."

GENUINE BOLDNESS

The power of boldness that I want you to harness involves more than just being comfortable meeting people. Genuine boldness means deciding to put yourself in situations that most people normally wouldn't. Shy behavior doesn't just keep us from saying things, but from doing things. Our hesitation, just like our reticence, ends up preventing us from having unique and satisfying experiences all the time. *In essence, boldness is simply moving from inaction to action.*

But that is a big move. Most people choose inaction. Most people stay in their comfort zone 24/7. It's a whole lot easier. But if you're dissatisfied with life so far, and want to discover what's really possible, you're going to have to make that crucial, simple move from inaction to action.

What I also want you to discover is that boldness is rewarded in unexpected ways. It's as if you radiate fearlessness, and the sea parts. Lieutenant Colonel Bill Kilgore, the character played by Robert Duvall in the movie *Apocalypse Now*, was based on real individuals. The way he would strut around fearlessly with bullets flying around him as everyone was diving for cover was not a fictional dramatization. Many soldiers in Vietnam talked about how some men just seemed invincible and acted that way. And nothing ever happened to them. Or was it the other way around? Was it their state of mind that made them invincible?

I'm not talking about being bulletproof in real life, but metaphorically I absolutely am.

Most people go through life dodging imaginary bullets, and most of the time nothing is aimed at them at all. Or is as harmless as a marshmallow.

This book is about discovering how to act boldly and feeling the thrill of it. And seeing the power of it. And the joy. And most of all, the fulfillment of your dreams and greater purpose.

And just so you know, I'm not talking about being obnoxiously bold, where people are grossly inconvenienced, or hurt, or seriously offended, or taken advantage of by what you say or do. The truth is that almost every action offends somebody.

You can be Mother Teresa and there will be someone who thinks you're an attention hog. I don't believe in giving those types of people a second thought. You might make people uncomfortable—which most of the time is their issue, not yours—but I'm not advocating rude or bad behavior. I sincerely believe you can be bold, polite, and considerate at the same time, and act with integrity in every situation. That to me is true fulfillment, to be your absolute boldest self while still having integrity in everything you do.

WHAT'S HOLDING YOU BACK?

Let's be honest: if developing boldness was easy, as easy as wishing it, you'd have done it a long time ago. But it's also true that many of you haven't tried.

I hear people resisting change all the time. "I hate change," they say, with great emphasis. "I just want things to stay the same." But what I see is people love change. We all love change. ATMs. Netflix. Smartphones. Facebook. Do you really want to start going back into banks for your money? Or using a big paper map to find directions? No anti-lock brakes, no internet, no arthroscopic surgery? Everything should stay exactly the same, right? I didn't think so.

Face it. You don't hate change at all. You just hate *to* change. It's really just you resisting changing yourself. The rest of the world better keep on improving. In fact, it's not just the world around you that needs to keep improving. *Other people* need to change too. We have self-improvement recommendations for everyone else. That guy in finance needs to learn to chill out. That gal at the bank needs to wise up before she gets herself fired. So-and-so needs to lose weight or he's going to have a heart attack. That lady needs to stop complaining and realize how good she has it. Those people need a better attitude. Sound familiar?

We just don't like the idea of changing *ourselves*. We get very attached to who we think we are, who we define ourselves as, much as it's mostly fiction and it's not even how most people see us. For example, we may think we come off as intellectual and clever, when we are actually regarded as sarcastic and snide. (That would be me, for thirty years or so!) Or we think we come off as quiet and reserved, when instead we are regarded as cold and aloof.

My point is, your definition of you and other people's perception of you are both wrong, and both can be changed. But the first step is saying, "I'm ready to change." I can do nothing for you until that moment, and I'm going to spend a good part of the beginning of this book getting you to say that and really mean it, and then together we will make everything happen.

Here are some things you might be telling yourself and that have become all-encompassing beliefs that hold you back from beginning your journey. I'm putting them down here, in black and white, so you can face them and move on.

"I Will Lose Myself"

As I present people with the possibility of becoming bolder, one of the classic defense mechanisms they default to is saying, "This just isn't me."

I immediately point out that when I talk about getting someone to say, "I want to change," I'm saying that I want them to change their *behavior*. It's almost impossible to "lose" who you are. The essential you is not going to be erased, no matter what you do. But we all can change and improve many aspects of our behavior. The happiest people do it throughout their entire lives.

If you see yourself as introverted, I'm sure you are quite capable of telling yourself and everyone else that you don't mind being that way: "It's just the way I am." But have you ever found yourself with a group of like-minded people, talking about a subject you are very interested in, and suddenly you are contributing eagerly, in an animated and excited way, perhaps even dominating the whole conversation? I'm sure that's happened at least once or twice. You know why it happened? Because you are not shy. You just don't know how not to *act* shy, so you define yourself that way.

Think of yourself like a song. A song doesn't have to be played just one way, or with one interpretation. The Beatles' song "Something" has been covered by more artists than any other song in history. Fast, slow, jazzy, rocking, but it's still *that* song. What we will be doing is creating variations of you, so to speak, with you being the theme, and the variations will be behavior that you *choose* for that situation rather than fall into.

Your song doesn't have to be monotonous, in its figurative meaning as well as literal. You can have many tempos, jump octaves, howl, whisper, and your rock opera will still be your own.

Who do you know who truly changed into someone else? I'm willing to wager no one. But at the same time, are you the same person you were in high school? In college? I'm certainly not. My basic personality is mostly the same. But I've become well-traveled. I've learned to sell, to be a businessman, to speak publicly. To discern colors even with my vision impairment. To control my anger, my profanity, my sarcasm, and a hundred other things over sixty years. I'm definitely still me, but I'm not at all the person I once was. And, by the way, I'm not who I will be. I'm making choices every day to grow, learn, and blossom in new ways. Still, nobody thinks I've become someone else.

From wherever you are on the boldness scale, you can choose to grow, advance, and elevate yourself to untold heights of boldness until you are superbold, summoning it whenever you choose. You'll still be that essential you. Just a more wonderful version.

"People Will Mock/Hate/Laugh at Me"

This is a big fear—and we don't just face these reactions from strangers. There are people you love who will try and deter you from boldness. They'll tell you that you shouldn't aim so high. They'll say they are trying to protect you from disappointment. In other words, they think you'll fail.

These people simply don't know that boldness is a superpower. They think ambition leads to failure and heartbreak. To that I say, so what? I've failed plenty, and I've had my heart broken more than a few times over the years. It didn't convince me that I don't want love in my life. It convinced me that I have to be a better person in the relationship and find someone who is a better match. That's all. Not crawl into a cave and die alone.

Those strangers who try and knock you down, who mock you, are not worthy of your attention or affection. Think about mockery. It's really just a form of bullying. Not a sign of intelligence, or anything positive, really. It's just insecurity perverted into hateful behavior. We see children and teenagers do it, and some of them carry it into their adult lives. They are to be pitied. Still, they can certainly harm you by embarrassing or humiliating you, and probably have.

It's time to change your thinking about them. Replace your resentment or hurt with pity. With empathy, even. There is no more unfortunate person in my mind than a bully. To try to make yourself feel good by making other people feel bad? By hurting people? How much lower a life form could you be?

"Screw All Them, Screw All That, I'm Moving On"

Later, I'm going to give you tools to deal with rejection and failure, including where those two feelings come from and how to change their meaning. But for now, I want to give you a simple piece of armor. It's a new message to tell yourself—a concise statement to reinforce the new mindset. When you're feeling mocked, or embarrassed, or unsteady, or people make you feel awkward, or you've talked yourself into feeling that way, this is what you say:

"Screw all them, screw all that, I'm moving on."

You don't say it out loud. And you don't say it angrily or with resentment. You say it to yourself in a lighthearted way. With a little shrug, maybe. And a hint of a smile.

As Taylor Swift would say, "Shake it off." Try saying it right now. You'll find it liberating, I believe. Sitting by yourself, think of some situation or someone that hurt you or mocked you. And now say it out loud: "Screw all them, screw all that, I'm moving on." Maybe say it a few times, until you really feel the lightness that comes from saying it. You may even start laughing at the fact that you let it bother you. Shout it out, if you are in a place where you can. See how it feels. Remember to smile as you do it. It adds a little magic.

I hope you're not offended by the language, but it's meant to be strong, memorable, and determined. This is your key mantra, your chant, your power refrain in dealing with those hurtful situations. In fact, if you so choose, change the word "screw" to the f-word. You won't be saying it out loud anyway, unless you're alone. It's for you, internally. Say whichever version works for you to feel empowered and to release the grip that others' opinions have on you.

Please don't see this mantra as an act of hostility toward people, because I NEVER want you to say it out loud to anyone. This is designed to jam the signal of hurt and rejection that you are perceiving, whether real or imagined, so you are not weakened by it, but rather strengthened. This is about self-preservation until you no longer need it, an invisible suit of armor that allows you to walk away unharmed.

Remember, this mantra is temporary—it's like training wheels. Bold people never have to do this. They already ignore rejection. They behave as if it doesn't exist, and therefore, for them, it doesn't. (I'll get you there, I promise!) This is why people often define them as charismatic. They don't have armor; they have an aura. An aura of superboldness.

For now, you must realize that most of the time, rejection is not about you. Even if sometimes it is, must everyone love you? Must everyone find you interesting? That's a tall order, a ridiculous need. Let *that* go, and you'll feel pretty powerful. You'll be looking for your people, your tribe. Nobody else is necessary.

"I Don't *Want* to Change—I'm Happy As I Am"

I'm not ruling out being an introvert as an effective lifestyle. I know a woman who is truly antisocial and she's also a great writer who cranks out a new novel every year. She probably has no need for this book, unless she decides she is unhappy with her social existence and realizes she is hiding and would rather stop writing and fall in love.

Maybe you are a software engineer on par with Mark Zuckerberg and have incredible focus because you have no social life, and that has made you a substantially more proficient programmer. You might not need this book either, because someone will find you and invest in you, or hire you, and someone with low intimacy needs will marry you for your brains and your money. And your life will be fine.

But if you're not one of these people, maybe you're just geeky and need to find ways to interact with people even as a geek. There is nothing wrong with being nerds or geeks, by the way. They are creating the new world. The problem is, it often makes you reticent, socially inept, and therefore unhappy.

As I said earlier, you won't lose you. Don't confuse your ingrained behavioral patterns with your true identity, the essential you. That's easy to do, and certainly an easy excuse to cling to when you're afraid of the risks of change and the uncomfortable feeling that goes with it. You are not defined by your past. You need to spend a little time getting beyond what you've constructed for the outside world to see and get down to who you are at your core. And more importantly, who you would become if you only could.

Don't trust your self-definition. Very few people besides you actually believe it, and you're letting it rigidly define you rather than continually evolving that definition of yourself. Those definitions that you believe are written in stone, that are the immutable "you"? They are not. They are written in rewritable code, and we're going to mess with that programming big-time.

Don't get me wrong. I know there are hidden advantages to being shy or introverted. When you're a friend, you're a really good friend. But often, you get too clingy and needy, and you end up overwhelming people who could be good friends, or who could enjoy you in smaller doses.

You also undoubtedly have learned other skills that you may not have if you had a robust social life. You might be an avid reader, or a *Jeopardy* master, or a skilled magician. You've had more alone time, and hopefully diverted your energy in productive ways, not just playing online poker or lurking on Instagram and TikTok.

That is not a judgment on my part. It is who you've come to be, and I want you to acknowledge it and decide if it's time to move beyond it. If you're a magician, it's time to perform for bigger audiences than your family. Or, if trivia is your skill, you need to try to get on a game show. If you're an engineer, it's time to start having sex.

If you have even the slightest suspicion that your life would be better if you were bolder, this book is for you.

WHAT THIS BOOK IS

I'm sure growing up, and perhaps even in adulthood, someone has told you, "Don't be shy." Or even better, "Don't be *so* shy!" That helped, didn't it? All you really needed was someone to tell you to stop so that you could blossom into the outgoing social butterfly you always wanted to be. As if. Or you were at a party and a friend said something like, "Just go up and talk to him (or her)!" Meanwhile, you're thinking, "If I could do *that*, then I wouldn't be standing here *not* doing it!"

I'm not going to be doing that. Instead, I'm going to give you a step-by-step method on how to go from wherever you might be on the shy/bold spectrum now to someone who can talk to strangers, speak up first, tell people what you expect from them, and generally be comfortable acting boldly in any situation. You may still *feel* shy, or at least have moments when you do, no matter what I teach you. But it will not be how you define yourself. I will show you how to do this through the PRIDE Method, which is divided into five steps:

1. **Preparation**—Things go a lot easier when you prepare, especially the initial words you want to say to someone.
2. **Relaxing**—There are simple ways that you can reduce your anxiety before and during any social encounter or endeavor.
3. **Insight**—You will come to understand the stories you tell yourself that create imaginary danger.
4. **Dosage**—Controlling the level of intensity of a social experience is key because everyone is different and has a different capacity,

and increasing that Dosage at the pace you can handle is essential to becoming bolder.

5. **Every Day Action**—The most essential step in bringing about change—any kind—is daily activity toward your goal.

These steps interact with each other to create genuine boldness. But you're not just going to take my word for it—you're going to practice the PRIDE Method in what I call the Boldness Exercises (or sometimes just exercises). These exercises are divided into five levels so that you can work your way up the shyness/boldness scale. Many of them—and much of the content in this book—is about the dynamics of meeting new people. The reason for this is that connecting with people in a meaningful way is the foundation for boldness, because becoming bold starts with an ability to meet anyone you want and to move through the world comfortably in any social situation. Your bold actions will flow from this capability.

Remember, these Boldness Exercises are training. The aim is to be superbold—bold at any moment you may need it. It might be helpful to think of the Boldness Exercises like playing scales when learning a musical instrument. They are not the whole song, just the keys that you will want to know how to play that sound best together. Like all new learning, we will start at a very basic level until you get the hang of it.

I will also explain the psychology of your under-confidence, and give you tools to help you move past it, such as Guiding Principles, Social Skills, and Power Tools. All of these will help you develop your boldness and hold on to it. And I'm going to ask that you keep a journal.

"Why a journal, Fred?" you're probably thinking. Because this book is about taking action. An essential part of that will be logging your results on a daily basis, so a journal is critical. I recommend making it a physical journal, with a nice cover on it, because this is your transformation manual, and you want it to be tangible. I do believe there is something about having a real object, a talisman symbolizing and empowering your growth and transformation. Keep it private. This is for your eyes only.

It has been demonstrated that writing things down is even more effective in moving ideas into your consciousness than typing but, if you absolutely must go digital, then use an app like Evernote so that you are putting everything in the right place and can access it anywhere.

Your Boldness Journal has two purposes: to track your progress, both the failures and the victories, and also to reflect on your past, for motivation to become even bolder. The more dedicated you are to the Journal Entries throughout this book, the faster you will progress in confidence, boldness, and fulfillment.

We start now with your first entry.

Journal Entry #1: Moments That Made a Difference

Looking at your life, you should be able to recall a few moments that were pivotal, that perhaps opened a new door for you or even pushed you into something that changed the course of your life. You've already heard one of mine: the time I spoke up in a pool hall and it led to a friendship with Gary and his two incredible sons.

I want you to recall those moments now because most often those were flashes of boldness, where you spoke up, or acted, didn't hesitate, and a surprising opportunity came your way. You may have had several of those moments, or just a few, or maybe only one. I hope at least one. Now, go to your journal and start a section called Moments That Made a Difference. Put down the incidents you can think of. Come back and add more if you think of them.

These moments of boldness are your touchstones. They remind you that you *can* be bold; you just need to practice it. Turn to them for courage and motivation as you expand your confidence and develop your superpower.

In your journal, write down the moments where you were bold and it changed your life. Keep adding to this list as you think of more.

READY FOR ACTION?

If you've succeeded at anything in life, it's most likely because someone somewhere along the line was hard on you. They didn't let you off the hook and let you settle for mediocrity. When it comes to you becoming superbold, that person is going to be me.

At first, we are going to take baby steps. For some of you, they may feel too slow. But starting this way forms a critical foundation, a template you will always be able to go back to and examine why you failed at an interaction, and how you could have improved it. We're also going to begin with exercises that very gradually increase your social abilities, expand your comfort zone, and heighten your boldness.

My goal is to do it at a pace where you can see the build of it, the progress, and get encouragement to step up a little more. If it feels slow for you, you can work through the Boldness Exercises faster until you hit your discomfort zone. Then slow down and refine your superpower. It's not about how fast or slow you do the exercises. It's about steady progress with no setbacks.

Don't expect it to happen overnight. But you will feel better every step of the way because you will learn how to change, gradually and permanently.

CHAPTER 2

WHY LISTEN TO ME?

Think you're shy? I'll probably top you in every category and on every occasion you've ever felt shy. Under-confident? Got you beat. Missed great opportunities? I could fill two books with mine. Here's a sample:

In high school, one time I missed my carpool ride, and one of the kids from my neighborhood was going to hitchhike, which I had never done. I couldn't imagine having the courage to just stick my thumb out and hope someone would give me a ride. Even worse, then I would have to talk to a complete stranger. Horrors. So I asked if I could tag along with him, and he agreed.

After several cars passed us by, my classmate said, "I think we'll do better if we split up." So he jogged fifty feet ahead, put his thumb out, and was picked up moments later. I spent the next two and a half hours walking home, never able to raise my thumb to a passing car.

I had such poor social skills I didn't know enough to apologize when I spilled my wine on my prom date's dress. (Pamela Childs, if you're out there,

I'm really sorry.) I wasn't exactly raised right. It really wasn't my upbringing so much as the effect of shyness on my simple courtesies. When it came to anything with an emotional charge to it, I couldn't speak up.

As I mentioned earlier, I was too shy to tell Robin Williams he was in two of my favorite movies. I was hanging out with him in a condo in Tahoe on a ski trip with friends. I couldn't vocalize a simple compliment in the most relaxed of circumstances.

Not to mention countless parties where I didn't meet a single new person. I was pretty much incapable of walking up to a woman I didn't know and starting a conversation with her.

Regrets, I've got a mountain of them.

I had a job where they wanted to promote me to sales from the stockroom because they thought I had promise. They sat me down at a desk and told me to start making phone calls to potential clients. I couldn't make a single phone call. Back to the warehouse I went.

Eventually, that changed. It was gradual, but I moved in fits and starts in the direction of boldness. I was rewarded more often than I was punished. Way more often.

This is who I've now become. I've done stand-up comedy. I've done improv comedy (which is like stand-up, but you go onstage without material!). I've spoken to audiences of over five thousand people. I have met and talked to dozens of celebrities. I've MC'ed two weddings. I've played chess with Sir Richard Branson. I've given heartfelt eulogies for my mother, my oldest friend, and my second father. I've acted in over one hundred TV commercials.

More importantly, I can also walk up to absolutely anyone, introduce myself, and have a cogent and pleasant conversation without babbling or getting tongue-tied. I can tell my lover what I want and how I feel. My friends and family know how much I treasure them. I can speak in front of thousands of people with joy, energized with adrenaline, and not paralyzed with fear. In other words, superbold.

I'm admired for my boldness as well as my achievements.

If I can do all this from where I started, you can too, and a whole lot faster than I did, because I've analyzed how I beat it and simplified and systematized the process for you.

Let me give you a detailed example of boldness in action.

Recently, there was a special meeting at a convention I was at, a dinner exclusively for CEOs of companies that I do business with. I was not invited, but there were a number of people I wanted to meet, so I walked into the cocktail party portion of the dinner. No one stopped me, and I didn't have a badge on to identify myself or say I belonged, and so I just started introducing myself.

These were all my disadvantages:

- I knew almost no one.
- I was not invited.
- I did not "belong" there; I wasn't a CEO in that segment of the industry.
- I was underdressed; most were in suits or jackets, and I was in casual attire.

Now don't get me wrong. I wasn't entirely comfortable. But I was *acting* like I was comfortable—smiling, introducing myself to people, connecting to them with my eyes and attention. And when someone who was in charge of the badges asked my name, I told her the truth, that I wasn't invited. She didn't ask me to leave, but told me that people would eventually sit down to eat, and they only had so many seats, and at that point I would have to leave. Later, as the cocktail party transitioned into a sit-down dinner, she came up to me and I thought, "OK, now I'm getting the boot!" Instead, she said, "Some people didn't show up for dinner, so you're welcome to stay."

This all happened because I followed one of my prime boldness rules: *always wait until someone else tells you that you can't; don't be the one to stop yourself.* If it's seriously important that you shouldn't be doing something or shouldn't be somewhere, someone will stop you. But that will usually be the worst of repercussions. Which means…NOTHING BAD HAPPENED!

That night I met several new business contacts, which was my goal. But if I had gotten thrown out, hey, I wasn't supposed to be there anyway, but at least I tried. Here is a critical point: as long as you don't register being told to leave somewhere as a negative thing, as long as you don't decide to experience it that way, it's actually a positive thing. It's an indicator that you found the true boundary.

That's an essential rule of boldness: **never be the one stopping you.**

MY CATALYST

So what changed me? How did I get out of my own way?

There were many moments in my life where I wished I'd been bold enough to act. Some were small and perhaps insignificant. But two I would call life-changing. These two incidents left the deepest impact, and they frustrated me to the point where I knew I had to change.

One was a woman with whom I hesitated to initiate a relationship. I look back now and it was so incredibly obvious that the opportunity was there, that she was open to it and was simply waiting for me to indicate my own interest. But my hesitance, my fear of rejection, silenced me. It held me back from expressing what was nearly bursting inside me. Years later I ran into a friend of hers who told me that this woman had gotten married but had confided to her that she once loved me and had always wished something had happened between us. It was one of the great mysteries of her life why it didn't.

Do I think she was the love of my life? No. I've managed to find love, deep love, more than once. But the painful truth is that I missed that chance *because of my shyness*. But had that not happened, had I not been so slain by the realization that we could have been together had I just spoken up, then maybe I would have kept bumbling along, missing one opportunity after another. I honestly look at that painful memory as a good thing, because the sting of it was so sharp that I vowed to change, to purge myself of my shyness and to somehow figure out how to act boldly and confidently.

The second happened many years later, when I was on vacation in China. I have a tendency to wander off the beaten tourist path when I'm traveling, especially if I'm feeling trapped within a tour group. We were in Beijing, and a few of us had migrated away from the rest of our tour mates. Most of them were meandering through a local open-air market, and four of us split off and headed down one of the dirt side roads into the town.

It was delightful. We were just taking in the remarkable differences in how people lived versus our own suburban lives. As we walked, we began to hear a loud clanging and eventually came upon a circle of men who were working with a forge out in the open air. As we watched, we realized they were blacksmiths. They were pulling out glowing-hot blades from a blazing forge and placing them on a wide anvil, and men two at a time were hammering the blade to temper it. After watching for a few moments, we saw that they were creating axe blades. Sparks were flying in the air, and the rhythmic music of the steel being pounded filled our ears. The hammering duo were perfectly synchronized, one striking and then recoiling just as the other struck, almost like a cartoon. It was fascinating.

I had the strongest urge to go up to them and ask if I could take a try at swinging one of the hammers. Of course, I spoke no Chinese. In other words, Shyness Excuse #1.

I could have easily made myself understood with gestures. But they probably wouldn't want me to ruin an axe, would they? Shyness Excuse #2.

Did I ask? No. I stood there, frozen to the ground. My whole spirit wanted to leap forward, but my entire nervous system, my damaged psyche, held me back. So I stood there and watched. Eventually, we walked away.

On that same trip, I saw the Great Wall of China—one of the Seven Wonders of the World—so immense you can see it from outer space. I stood in Tiananmen Square, where all those years ago a young man stood defiantly in front of a Chinese tank in that iconic photograph. I saw the Forbidden City. Later in the trip we drove across the vastness of the Tibetan plateau, with the Himalayas in the background, where few Americans have ever walked. But you know what I remember most about that whole vacation? Not asking if I could swing that hammer.

When I got home from that trip, haunted by that memory, I decided that I would never be that guy again. I was never going to be the one to tell myself no. I was never going to be the one to miss an amazing opportunity.

Imagine if I had done it. That would have been a remarkable memory, a true, once-in-a-lifetime moment. And not just for me, but for those Chinese blacksmiths too. Some crazy American wants to take a whack at that anvil—they'd have been talking about it for the rest of their lives. All of us would have gotten a rare memory out of it.

I believe now that those blacksmiths would have let me do it. But even in the unlikely chance that they shooed me away, I still wouldn't have the nagging memory of *not asking*, and I would be fine, because at least I would have tried.

The fact is, no matter what they said, I would not have died of embarrassment or rejection. This is important to note. Trying and failing feels infinitely better than being too shy to try. In fact, I've come to believe that trying and failing at those kinds of things is a positive experience—the reward is in the attempt.

That was the second big catalyst for me. I became determined to never be that guy again. I was not going to listen to those self-authored excuses. And I'm certain of one thing: if I were me, the *me* I have become, I *know* they would have let me swing that hammer.

How many of those moments do you have? Reflect on those and write some down in your journal.

Journal Entry #2: My Missed Opportunities

List a time when you hesitated and the moment passed, when you could have met someone, introduced yourself, said something good, or been helpful or encouraging, or taken a big risk. Write them here whenever you recall another one. Then also add:

- What did you miss out on?
- What could you have said or done?
- What difference would that have made in your life?

Highlight when someone gave you a golden opportunity, laid it right out in front of you, and you still missed it.

Go to your journal now and list the opportunities you missed, the ones you regret the most.

How many more is it going to take before you decide that's not who you want to be, that you don't want to miss one more moment, one more opportunity? That's when your best life can truly begin.

I know that sounds extreme, but I believe that many parts of your life, of your honest pursuit of happiness, are on hold because of a lack of boldness when it matters most. I hope I can get you as frustrated as I was, because then you're ready.

Once you're bold, there's no going back. You'll realize that other person wasn't you at all. It was a disguise you were wearing, a mask you hid behind. Or worse, a prison of your own making, a cage you forged with your inhibiting stories. Even if you didn't build it yourself, you're locked in it.

This book is about giving you a combination to that lock. Don't believe for a second that the real you is not trying to get out, trying to lead the greatest possible life, with the most love, the most impact, the most fulfillment. You may have suppressed it, but it didn't make you any happier, just safer.

To begin unlocking your cage, you must begin with *awareness*. You need to learn *how* the cage was built, how you got this way, so you can begin questioning those assumptions. That's what the next chapter is about. We'll explore the processes, thoughts, and instincts that make and reinforce your under-confidence so that you see how the PRIDE Method and the tools in this book will help you.

There's a saying, "The safest place for a ship is in the harbor, but that's not what they were built for." Same for human beings. We're meant to strain ourselves, to grow, get stronger by pushing our boundaries. If we don't, we atrophy, socially, mentally, and physically. And it's a lousy way to go.

CHAPTER 3

HOW YOU GOT THIS WAY

"There are three kinds of people in the world:
those that made it happen,
those that watched it happen,
and those who wonder what happened."

—Tommy Lasorda, LA Dodgers manager

What do you believe has most held you back in achieving your goals and dreams? Think carefully about this. Where would you put the blame? Was it your gender? Your parents? Your education? Maybe it was your race, your ethnicity, or your accent. How about the economy, the government, or the competition? Or was it your IQ, your height, or the shape of your head?

Here's the real answer: what holds you back most are the stories you tell yourself. Specifically, the stories you tell yourself about what you *can't do.* Think about it: no one talks to you more than you do. And you're stuck listening to those same messages over and over again. If something is repeated long enough and we trust the speaker (it is you, after all), then it becomes a belief, and then, because we've believed it long enough, we make it the truth.

That's what we will explore in this chapter: the social conditioning and stories that have led you to where you are. It's crucial to understand these beliefs before we dig into the practical tools and methods to help you outgrow your confidence limitations. The first step toward change is always self-awareness. And that can be painful. Most people don't enjoy taking a hard look at their faults or examining how the choices they've made have limited their lives and their happiness. It's a whole lot easier to blame outside forces for your limitations. But it doesn't get rid of them. In fact, it makes them permanent.

It's time to change that, starting with Doctor No.

DOCTOR NO AND BARRIER BELIEFS

Tragically, it is mostly our own voice telling us what we can't do and who we can't be. Throughout our lives, we add to a list of definitions about ourselves, and then we have an inner voice repeating these messages. You may have heard it referred to as self-talk, or your inner critic. I call it *Doctor No.* The doctor who's always telling you the worst-case scenario, under the guise of "protecting you from being hurt."

I've heard Tony Robbins talk at length about this self-programming. He makes the distinction between *limiting beliefs* that hinder us and hold us back and *empowering beliefs*, which strengthen us, motivate us, and give us confidence. He didn't discover this behavior and is not the only one pointing it out. But he articulates it extremely well and does a very good job of releasing people from those negative messages.

I'm going to refer to those negative messages as *barrier beliefs* because these beliefs have become solid prison walls that prevent you from reaching your dreams. If you've never heard this behavioral truth before, I hope it resonates with you. If you have, I'm sure that you, like all of us, need reminding of it, because sadly, we are all highly skilled at maintaining our barrier beliefs. Here are some typical messages from Doctor No:

"I'm not good at math."

"I can't sing a note."

"I'm no dancer."

"I'm not good with names."

"I don't make friends easily."

"I'm not funny."

"I'm not social."

"I don't open up easily."

"People don't like me right away."

"I'm bashful."

"I prefer to be alone."

"I don't need a lot of friends."

"I don't need attention like some people."

"I don't have time to meet new people."

"I hate selling."

"I'm terrified of speaking in public."

"People are just escaping their responsibilities with social frivolity."

"I don't need everyone to love me."

"I'm not a show-off."

"I'm shy."

How many people are saying these exact words to themselves and to others? Ever heard yourself say any of these about yourself? These barrier beliefs are like an electrified fence we've erected around ourselves, keeping the fun out. I look at it like lines of software code, our personal social program that we turn into the "truth" about who we are. We act reflexively and consistently based on those lines of code.

Let's take just one of those, math. The fact is that most people aren't naturally bad at math. They just missed a few lessons along the way, and because mathematics is an *accretive learning process*—which means that everything new builds on what you've already learned—it becomes almost impossible to progress, and so we hate math because we're "bad" at it, meaning we've stacked up a few failures, missed a few key steps, and now Doctor No steps in with the diagnosis, "You're not good at math."

There are brilliant educational sites like the Khan Academy (www.khanacademy.com), where you only advance to the next lesson once you've successfully completed and understood the previous lesson. Students who do that succeed and learn to love math (and other subjects as well). Math is actually easy to love, because it is one of the most predictable things is life. Four times five is always going to be twenty, and the circumference of a circle will always be its diameter times pi. Not much else in life adds up like math.

But if you tell yourself often enough that you're bad at math, you'll not only believe it, you will eventually make it true. Which in the context of becoming bold is a real problem because your self-definition about your social behavior and tendencies have also become true. We've got to address that head-on because if you're not good at math, your phone has a calculator. But if you've convinced yourself that you're not interesting or that people don't like you right away, the only option is to fix yourself.

The PRIDE Method and the Boldness Exercises employ this exact accretive learning principle. You will work your way up gradually, systematically, step-by-step, to greater and greater boldness. In the process, you'll erase a lot of lines of bad code and silence Doctor No.

Bold people define themselves with positive code and add new lines of code to their social software all the time, expanding their skills, their social circle, and their comfort zone.

Doctor No has other messages too. They are warnings, most often, and sound like this:

- I can't do this.
- I'm not good enough.
- People don't find me interesting.
- I'm not worth people's attention.
- I'm not appealing.
- I'm not cool enough for these people.
- I don't fit in with these kinds of people.
- I'm going to get my feelings hurt.
- This could go very badly.
- This will be embarrassing.
- People will laugh at me.
- People can't be trusted.
- I'd rather be alone.

Doctor No will also give ample detail as to the particulars. Like who specifically might not be interested in you. Or what types of people find you boring. Or where you won't be accepted. Or how painful the failure will be. And you believe it.

For now.

As we progress, we are going to be creating your Doctor Yes, who will give you messages that are entirely the opposite of what you've been telling yourself. Your self-talk will never stop, but we can change the messages, and you will be astounded at the result. I don't expect you to be convinced of that right now, but six months from now, you won't need convincing because the evidence will be everywhere.

Being bold won't make you into someone else, much as you will try to tell yourself that barrier belief too. It will make you unstoppable. Do not doubt for one second that you can become that. Do not doubt for one second that a day will come when you will be challenged, and it will be the crucible that determines how you regard yourself from that day forward. That may sound dramatic, and I mean it to be.

It won't just be that you are able to speak your mind. When you can speak your mind, you can also *act* boldly. I've watched a small woman stand up to a big, domineering man and make him back down. I've seen authority figures put in their place. I've watched former wallflowers wade into a group of people and make half a dozen friends in thirty minutes.

To get there, you're going to have to make some essential shifts in mindset. If you've learned anything from "Doctor No and Barrier Beliefs," it should be this: "Don't believe everything you think."

Journal Entry #3: My Barrier Beliefs

To eradicate these thoughts, you first need to list them. In your journal, list all the things Doctor No has told you on a daily basis. These will be the excuses, rationalizations, and stories you tell yourself, those negative lines of code that you believe define you.

Write down what you can think of right now. You won't be able to catch them all, but you'll catch some. From now on, every time you hear yourself say a discouraging thing, a limiting belief, or an excuse why you won't attempt something, write it down here.

Later you'll come back and read them and see how wrong or misguided or just plain inaccurate they were. Especially after you've had some success with the Boldness Exercises. Some will seem absolutely crazy, and others you will still have to attack.

Make your journal entry listing all the barrier beliefs you can think of, and add to it whenever you think of another.

NATURE, NURTURE, AND CONFORMING

While it's important to accept responsibility for how we think and recognize our power to change it, Doctor No was not created in a vacuum. A lot of our barrier beliefs have been shaped by social programming, and they block our natural tendency to be social.

Human beings are naturally, biologically social animals. It's how the human race has thrived and dominated the planet for the past hundred thousand years. Our proliferation as a species has been based almost entirely on successful tribal behavior. The concept of the "loner" and the "rugged individualist" came along much later, and the real versions of those were and are few and far between, despite how many people currently view themselves as that. Humans have always lived in communities, and it was the rare individual who could survive alone or would even try to. What that means is being introverted means you actually have to suppress your natural social needs and responses. Crazy, but true.

We are meant to interact with each other. Many anthropological studies show that people are much happier in communities, even primitive ones, and though modern civilization has allowed us to successfully isolate ourselves and still survive, it hasn't made us happier. Suicide rates are up, depression is rampant, and social media is not solving it. Perhaps it's even exacerbating it, because people are hiding inside their phones even when they are together.

I also don't mean you can't be happy spending time alone, so please don't twist my words. I think it's also essential to spend time alone, but it should be a choice.

To illustrate this, you may have noticed that kids love talking to strangers, until they suddenly reach an age when they don't. Recently, I was in a restaurant and sitting next to me was a young couple and their four-year-old daughter. At one point the little girl simply turned and introduced herself to me. She told me her age and her name, without being asked. Even spelled it for me: E-M-I-L-Y.

She did it very naturally, and it was very sweet. But I know that someday soon, she'll suddenly decide to act shy and stop being so friendly. Fortunately, I didn't see her parents discouraging her, so maybe she has a chance to retain her social boldness. Was I offended that she talked to me out of the blue, unprompted? No. Of course not. Obviously, her being a child, and a delightful one, made a difference.

So how did we lose our natural boldness? Think of children like Emily. I've seen a five-year-old child walk onto an airplane and say hi to everyone as they stroll down the aisle, while other children hide behind their mother's leg at the first hint of eye contact with a stranger. Why is this? How is one child so uninhibited and the other not? My answer is the second child was taught to be shy.

It is often the case that extroverted parents create introverted children and vice versa. Extroverts have a great deal of trouble identifying with the strong resistance that shyness creates, and as parents they force extroverted behavior on their children, only to drive them deeper into introversion. When this happens, I see self-confidence diminish because the young person sees himself "failing" socially in his parents' eyes.

This is not the intended result, of course. I have also seen some parents who don't want their children to outdo them in any way, and they will work at crushing the child's confidence. I find this sad, but it also makes me angry because it is so unloving and cruel.

And other parents—a much larger group than the last one I mentioned —simply have a negative or limited view of life's possibilities and opportunities, so they discourage the child, ostensibly because they want the child to "be realistic." They don't want their child to be hurt by the cold, cruel world out there, so they warn them to expect it. They try to get their child to conform.

This is important because it reinforces what I said at the beginning of this section: most of us became the way we are by social programming. Some of our behavior is genetic, of course, but we all danced and sang as children. We laughed and played and had to be told not to talk to strangers. And then someone told us about "show-offs" and made it clear how bad that type of person was. They told us to be quiet. Or they laughed at us, mocked us, made us feel self-conscious, made us feel embarrassed, or told us to grow up. To behave. To not stand out. To blend in.

None of that built boldness. They were only forces that eroded it. Society in general is very focused on messages that discourage boldness. The result is we spend a huge amount of time worrying about conforming. It's a big deal. But you must question this. Do we need to not be noticed? To not stand out? Why is that so bad? We are taught that it is rude, egotistical, improper socially, whatever. Conforming for those reasons brings up the question, "Who benefits when I conform?" The answer is "Someone else." Namely, the person who is getting the attention.

Attracting attention could result in a raise, a promotion, a date, a connection, or some other achievement. Why shouldn't you be pursuing these things? You're holding back so someone else can win the benefits of attention. Also, nonconforming doesn't really hurt anyone. Sure, it might make them uncomfortable, but comfort is overrated, and making strangers comfortable doesn't pay well unless you are a hotel employee or an anesthesiologist. Are you one of those? If not, forget about it.

A huge part of why we conform is fear. Our parents feared we would be rejected if we lived outside the bounds of "acceptable behavior," and then we began to fear it too. We need to fear less, not of things that are actually physically dangerous, but those that are actually harmless. I'm not trying to convince you to become a BASE jumper or snake handler. But you must become fearless of the harmless. Yes, to stop fearing things that actually can do you no harm unless you choose to let them!

For now, all you need to keep in mind is this: you will get there. I can't emphasize this enough. You will get there, just like someone with determination can lose one hundred pounds, if they have the right technique, the right system, and consistent behavior. This will be the same process for you, and a lot more fun than losing one hundred pounds, I assure you.

CRUTCHES

Doctor No and our desire to conform create "crutches" so that we can protect ourselves. We all have our own crutches, which are behaviors that protect us emotionally, get us through our day, and make us feel good about ourselves. Many are not particularly healthy, positive, or socially advantageous. Indeed, all they help us do is ignore the root of the problem and make us feel better about self-sabotaging behaviors. Some examples of crutches might be:

- Sarcasm
- Judgment
- Criticism
- Aloofness
- Coldness
- Rudeness
- Seclusion
- Video games
- Online gambling
- Offline gambling
- Working obsessively
- Alcohol
- Recreational drugs
- Porn

The problem is, we all want to be good at something. It's a natural desire. For some of us, it's painful not to be good at the thing we are attempting or what we hope to be good at, or well-known for, or appreciated for. We want instant success because the pain of failure means someone might be laughing at us, judging us, or critiquing us, and we can't stand that. So, we use these crutches to feel important or superior, or to dull the pain of not chasing our dreams.

Conversely, bold people love it when someone laughs at their mistakes, their missteps, and their faux pas. They are not afraid to look stupid, awkward, out of place, or incapable. It actually encourages them, letting them know they are one step closer to what they want to achieve. In the bold person's mind, missteps are really steps up. Plus, they know it makes them appear more vulnerable and more human. And they like that. They don't expect to be perfect, and they don't need to hide behind the illusion that they are. This is why we see them as charismatic. Everything seems to bounce off them.

Shy people delude themselves into thinking that instant perfection is possible because they don't want to fail, or be embarrassed, or make a mistake in front of anyone. That's just misguided. Even if someone thinks you're stupid, it doesn't make you stupid. Each one of us has our own level of intelligence. People's opinions don't move your IQ up and down—just your self-esteem. So, letting others affect your self-esteem is, well, stupid. And hey, maybe you are stupid. But I highly doubt it. Stupid people are not famous for overthinking things. Introverted people, on the other hand, are masters of it.

The crutches you use are a serious thing to reflect upon, and I don't mean to be flippant about it, because I know how ingrained they are and how safe they make you feel. But I also know what a threat they are to your happiness. I'm being a little sarcastic, to make it sting enough so that you examine yourself and where you are in this transition.

Journal Entry #4: My Crutches

Take a few minutes and write in your journal the crutches you think you use.

For example, being a critic is a great defense mechanism. You can criticize anything, have a strong feeling about unimportant things, dig a moat around yourself and your fiercely held, random opinions, whether they be about music, movies, actors, politicians, or whatever inspires your attack. And it feels kind of good. But where does it get you? Are you being paid to be a critic? Then fine. But if not, then I ask again, where does it get you? You're like a dog barking from deep inside his doghouse, afraid to come out and play in the yard.

Negativity may be the biggest waste of life that I've encountered. Believing in the worst, focusing on the bad side of everything, the expectation that things will go wrong or turn out badly, achieves only one thing: you're never going to be disappointed. Wow. What an accomplishment. A life to be proud of. (See? I've mastered sarcasm too!)

If this is you, and we all have this to some degree, being negative will stop you from enjoying almost everything. For example, who is better off? The person who laughs at the comedian with the average jokes, or the person who sneers at them? Who had a better time? Whose spirit was lifted?

I'm not saying you have to be positive about everything or like everything. I just want you to catch yourself if you have a mean-spirited opinion that doesn't really merit expressing. This behavior is often how the desperately lonely seek out someone they can be desperately lonely together with, by expressing an "Us vs. Them" philosophy or "The World Sucks" mindset. Or just finding fault with anyone successful.

I'll tell you one of my greatest personal crutches: I would point out my negative observation about someone rather than compliment them. I went to a high school where cutting people down was an art form. It did not prepare us well for society, especially me. I actually never learned how to compliment someone. At a certain point, I realized you have to put the nasty jibes away because what you've done is wrap yourself in barbed wire and you are prickly when you think you are being clever. It was a prison of negativity.

It didn't make me happier at all to be negative, by the way. I'm lucky to have the good friends that I do, who understood me and accepted me for who I was, which was deeply flawed.

Your crutches may be different, but I suspect you cling to them pretty tightly. If we put half the energy into refining our social skills that we put into telling ourselves false stories and excuses and spewing negativity, we'd probably become so happy that people wouldn't recognize us.

Remember, the author of these excuses knows their audience really well, knows exactly what is most persuasive and what their audience is blind to. You are the author and the audience is you. (I'm not sure I needed to point that out.) But you see why it's so effective? *You know exactly what will convince you most easily not to take action, so you fashion your whole argument around what persuades you best.* This is what I mean about a prison of your own making. Positivity unlocks the door.

Add your crutches to your journal. List as many as you can think of.

DIMENSIONS OF UNBOLDNESS

Now that you understand the concepts that reinforce your under-confidence, I want you to clearly assess where you are. Remember I said that in any given situation, you either acted boldly or you didn't? You may not exhibit shy behavior—or unboldness, as I will sometimes call it —all the time. There are different degrees of shy behavior and different dimensions of confidence and boldness. Some are situational, and some define our behavior entirely.

I want you to think about your present starting point, knowing that each step forward is an act of boldness. I'm going to define some of these dimensions of unboldness, and you can decide where you think you fit.

Paralyzing shyness. You avoid meeting new people. You actually can't speak in certain social situations. You become mute. You also cannot physically move in the direction of the conversation you want to join. Your brain keeps repeating over and over what you would like to say or do, but your body stays in the same position, glued to the ground.

Painfully shy. When encountering strangers, you generally don't speak until spoken to. You almost never bring up what you want in a situation, or if you do, you do it after everyone else has, and most likely agree with them rather than voice your own feelings or opinions. You have never done karaoke, asked a stranger for directions, or been the first person in the relationship to say, "I love you." You don't express appreciation even when you feel it. Someone at work says hi to you in the hall and you say hi back, but it's not audible. You seldom make eye contact.

Crowd shy. You don't feel comfortable in large groups of people. It overwhelms you as a social situation, and you avoid it at all costs. This is clinically called agoraphobia and some people genuinely have it, but many people are just shy around a concentration of strangers and are unable to mingle, blend in, or feel comfortable.

Fun shy. You won't let yourself have fun, even when everyone around you is. You are above it somehow. You are the proverbial wet blanket. No amount of encouragement gets you to join in. You are merely an observer. And often, you regret it later.

Singly shy. You can handle groups of people, but one-on-one, you've got no jam. You clam up, feeling every second of silence that passes is like five minutes. You look in different directions, hoping the other person will say something, but hopefully not walk away, and maybe someone will approach and initiate a conversation. Even with people you know well, when you are alone with them, in a car, for example, you can have long, painful silences. You avoid playing certain sports because you might need a partner or teammate, whether it's tennis, basketball, or rock climbing. First dates terrify you.

Creatively shy. You believe you are not talented enough to offer anything to anyone. You create but never offer to show it or perform for people. When asked to show your work or perform, you decline, playing it safe.

Public-speaking shy. You have stage fright, and it starts at around three people. This is the most prevalent form of unboldness. And in this day and age, when you need this skill just to survive in the business world, it is a serious impediment, with a real price tag.

Opposite-sex shy. (Or same sex, if that's your inclination.) You have zero social skills when you find someone attractive. You miss obvious cues when a person is interested in you. You've never made the first move.

Sales shy. You hate the idea of selling. You would fail at it if you tried, because you would either have to make cold calls or eventually ask for the order or some other terrifying act.

Shy when the stakes are high. You are confident socially and in most situations, except when it matters most. When the stakes are high, when it's important to you, you falter. The net result is the same:

you don't get to do or be who you want. You miss out on key moments, opportunities, and relationships, despite your normal confidence.

Be honest and find yourself on this list. (You may have two or three in combination.) Also understand that it doesn't matter where you are now. Remember, boldness can be learned. Certainly, some of us were born naturally bolder than others. But just as people are gifted at playing certain musical instruments, almost anyone can learn to play the guitar or piano with enough effort. Maybe not concert-level ability, but enough so you could enjoy yourself and play in a local band if you felt like it. Boldness is exactly the same.

Do I think everyone needs to be bold and outgoing? No. But if you want to be *more* bold, *more* outgoing, *more* relaxed, *more* comfortable in most social situations, the tools in this book will help you. How high on the boldness scale you go is really up to you. The sky is no limit. I am still expanding my boldness even now. Most of the first few decades of my life were wasted with rationalizations, self-doubt, social inadequacies, and hesitations—all the things I'm going to save you from so that your experience of true boldness will take months rather than years.

Maybe you're not painfully shy, but you're not as bold as you would like to be. Whatever your starting point on the boldness scale, I can take you higher. I want you to discover for yourself that boldness is a key that doesn't just unlock doors; it creates new ones. I firmly believe that you will eventually abandon unboldness as a lifestyle choice and fully embrace boldness. But for now, let's just set the goal closer by moving you up a few degrees. That's really how the Boldness Exercises work, as you will see.

MOVING BEYOND YOUR COMFORT ZONE

Before we end this chapter and move on to the PRIDE Method, I want to explore the concept of your comfort zone and its counterpart, your discomfort zone.

Human beings have a strong need to belong. Yet we also have a strong need to be unique. You will see average people do all sorts of things to appear unique, whether it's a Hell's Angels jacket or a Chanel handbag, a snake tattoo, or nose piercings.

We have a desire to attract attention, to feel some level of significance, at least in one tribe, however small. Tattoos and piercings are no different than Armani suits and Jimmy Choo shoes. They're both just costumes for different tribes. It makes me think of the expression, "Be a nonconformist; everyone is doing it." These serve as a way to identify someone in your tribe. These are people in your *comfort circle*. There is no social risk being taken. You are conforming by being unique within the tribe's parameters.

This comfort circle is very important to us, but we are going to redefine it and repurpose it. Right now, it serves as a great place to hide, to feel safe, not at risk of embarrassment, or failure, or challenge.

I'm not saying don't have a comfort circle. I have one, and it is a great gift in my life. But don't hide there. Just like you can't stay in bed all day, resting up for the challenges you are unwilling to face. As we progress through the exercises, your comfort circle is there to refresh you, relax you, and rejuvenate you so you can go back out and face the hard, rewarding challenge of chasing your dreams as you become bolder.

Venturing out of your comfort zone and into your discomfort zone can seem tough. In fact, there are specific words people use with themselves to prompt inaction, like *hard*, *difficult*, and *painful*. But the fact is, *hard* is neither good nor bad. *Difficult* is neither good nor bad. *Painful*, in fact, is neither good nor bad. They are just situations or conditions we all face at one time or another, willingly or unwillingly. It's how we label them that changes them.

For example, ask anyone if they want to get hit in the face or slammed into by someone running at them full steam. They would say, "No! That's crazy!" Except, people play sports all the time and get punched or slammed hard, in boxing or playing football, for example. They don't complain, but rather, they embrace it. It makes them feel alive. They've recategorized it as positive.

You can just as easily say, "This really hurts. I'm not doing this sport anymore," or "Wow, my shoulder is killing me. I must really be alive to feel this much pain." And get back on the field.

You just put a positive meaning to pain, which most people would choose to label as bad. Become conscious of how you label things, and see if they amount to more prescriptions from Doctor No.

In the alternative, I'm going to get you to label some different things as bad, like:

- Easy stuff
- The safe path
- The comfortable life
- Low-risk choices

This is the reality that you will discover as you become bolder. Your comfort zone can be a danger zone. It can trap you in inertia and keep you from taking action.

This is the big question: do you want to be a contender or a bystander?

Do you want to observe life through screens and audience seats, or do you want to build up the strength to step into the ring and come out swinging, and occasionally be victorious, a contender, someone who left it all on the mat?

We admire boxers because they willingly take beatings that we would never subject ourselves to. And they beat an opponent in the process because they don't just take a beating, they give one back. So, *if life is giving you a beating, maybe it's time to give one back.*

Sir Richard Branson, the founder of the Virgin empire, relates how his mother, Eve, told him when he was very young, "Some people watch other people do stuff. We do stuff." And so, he's had an entire life of bold actions, from hot-air ballooning across the Atlantic to launching a commercial space program with Virgin Galactic. He's no bystander.

Even if you don't always win in life—and you'll never win all the time—I guarantee you'll feel a whole lot more like a winner as a contender than as a bystander. To be a contender, it takes training, but it first takes saying, "I'm willing to be uncomfortable. I'm willing to endure the pain to get stronger, to be better, to push my boundaries."

Leave it all on the mat, and you'll die happy. That's what bold people do.

This means you'll have to venture outside of your comfort zone. That's the place where you stop feeling safe, and your body starts telling you you're in danger.

All the Boldness Exercises will be ventures into your *discomfort zone*. What will happen is your comfort zone will also get bigger and bigger as you get bolder and bolder. It happens imperceptibly at first, but once you look back, you'll see you've come a great distance and that the journey was difficult, painful, and delicious.

Now that you have a better understanding of where you are, how you got here, and what's been holding you back, let's look at what it will take to break down these barriers. Awareness is always the first step, but now you need to take action. That's where the PRIDE Method comes in. Ready for that first venture into your discomfort zone? Then let's begin!

PART II

THE PRIDE METHOD

CHAPTER 4

THE PRIDE METHOD: OVERVIEW

In this chapter, I will describe the steps of the **PRIDE Method**, the science behind why it works, and what you can expect once you start implementing this method. Then, in the chapters that follow, I will dive deeper into each stage, explaining how each one is critical and how they build on each other.

As I explained in Chapter 1, the PRIDE Method is a series of steps you can execute to act boldly. Each of these steps will help you move into your boldness without fear and actually *act*, no matter what the situation and what you want to do. You'll see the PRIDE Method in action in Part IV, when we dive into the Boldness Exercises; you'll be using this method as part of doing each exercise.

But first, you need to understand what the PRIDE Method is and how it works. I want you to think of the PRIDE Method as a matrix, each step reinforcing the other, sometimes done in sequence, other times essential in making each of the other steps work. If that's confusing, don't worry. You'll understand better what I mean as you do the exercises.

OVERVIEW

Once again, these are the steps of the PRIDE Method:

Preparation

Relaxing

Insight

Dosage

Every Day Action

Step 1: Preparation

As the first step of the PRIDE Method, Preparation is the foundation for everything going forward.

Preparation does something very important: it reduces anxiety. And anxiety is the main emotional driver behind shyness, hesitation, and reticence. That's why we start there.

At its most basic, Preparation is simply planning ahead of time what you are going to say before you meet someone, or what exactly you're going to do. Oddly, we prepare for all sorts of things in life, many of them not important, and then we don't prepare at all for many things that are much more important. We go to driving school, but no one teaches us how to shake hands or look someone in the eye. We learn language in detail —conjugations, vocabulary, pronunciation—and yet we are never taught basic courtesy, how to ask for help, how to introduce ourselves to a stranger, or how to nurture self-confidence. These are important life skills. That's what the Preparation stage of the PRIDE Method deals with: it gives you all the tools to prepare you for your bold actions.

Step 2: Relaxing

It's amazing what we can do in a relaxed state of mind, and equally amazing how much anxiety can impair our memory and our mental processing, and alter our facial expressions and body language.

People who have memorized speeches, musical pieces, or presentations and have learned them backward and forward can get in front of an audience, and suddenly their memory fails them. They can't access the information that was burned in just a few minutes earlier. They make mistakes, they stutter, their voice cracks, they sweat profusely. Why? Simply because people are looking at them.

Why does that matter so much?

Because we don't know how to relax. No one teaches this in school. Just as people say, "Don't be shy," they say, "Just relax," but they don't tell you how. I'm going to teach you how. It's really not that complicated. Remember that I said the PRIDE Method is a matrix? Preparation is part of what helps to relax you, and Insight also helps to relax you. But you need some very simple and basic physical techniques to finish the job.

The key ones are quite simple: breathing and changing your posture. We'll go into how to utilize them in detail, as well as a few other tricks. You'll be surprised at the difference it makes. Your words will come out. Your memory will work. Your body will exude confidence. And those ventures outside your comfort zone will become glorious adventures.

Step 3: Insight

Much of our behavior is controlled by our barrier beliefs, by the ever-present voice of Doctor No. These beliefs inhibit us from taking action and are the reinforcements to hesitation and reticence that are holding us back from realizing our maximum boldness.

I'm going to list the key insights that will improve your ability to Relax; they will also become part of your Preparation, because you will need to remind yourself of them when you find yourself unable to act or make the move you want to. These insights will also provide the motivation to act boldly, because they will reveal doors that you didn't think were open and opportunities that you didn't think were possible.

I will list them here, and you will find them repeated and expanded upon throughout the book.

Insight #1. People are not thinking about you anywhere near as much as you think they are. They are giving you a few moments' thought, and then they go back to thinking about themselves.

Insight #2. In reality, you are almost never in real danger. It just feels like you are. Your body is reacting that way, but it's a psychological misinterpretation of the situation.

Insight #3. It's time to start listening to Doctor Yes. Doctor No is feeding you false information. A lot. Those beliefs need to be recorded over with useful, positive messages. Don't believe everything you think, remember? Start to create the opposite messages for yourself.

Insight #4. You need to give yourself permission to have the life you want. You are the one holding you back most. Within this is the growing understanding that a lot of the really great stuff in life only happens when you venture into your discomfort zone. I repeat this key point we covered in Chapter 3: your comfort zone can be a danger zone.

Bold people understand all of these insights, and they are the foundation for their satisfying approach to life.

Step 4: Dosage

Specifically, this step means you are controlling the Dosage—the intensity —of whatever you set out to experience outside your comfort zone.

Here is a simple truth that many people don't consciously understand: *All of life is about Dosage.* Whether we're talking about food, drugs, stress, or the air we breathe, whether something makes you healthier, does nothing, or kills you—all of this is a matter of Dosage. Not enough of something and you starve or die. Too much and you become addicted and/or die. For example:

- **Oxygen.** It's a poison if it goes much beyond 50 percent of the atmosphere. But try going below 10 percent. You're dead.
- **Fast food.** Eat it once in a while, you just feel crappy. Eat it every day, you become obese, diabetic, and eventually dead.
- **Exercise.** Do it with too little weight or exertion and nothing happens. Try to lift too much, your muscles tear and your back will go out.
- **Stress.** We absolutely need some levels of stress in our lives, but we can only handle so much. Our brains, our muscles, even our emotions all get stronger from the right levels of stress.
- **One sleeping pill.** Helpful, but a whole bottle can be fatal.
- **Two aspirin.** Helpful, but a whole bottle can be fatal.

For some people, *one* aspirin equals dead because we all have different levels of tolerance. We need to figure out—actually, you do—the levels you can tolerate on your path to confidence, boldness, and fulfillment. You are not looking for the minimum, but rather the most you can handle. Because too little and nothing changes. Too much and there will be setbacks or abandonment of the path.

The principle of Dosage is the same as in medicine, where you inoculate yourself with a mild form of the disease to create resistance to it. You will be doing the same thing with uncomfortable experiences, building up your tolerance so that when you are chasing your dreams, you are strong enough and bold enough to take action, rather than hesitating or retreating.

Step 5: Every Day Action

When you work toward any goal by doing something every day toward achieving it, there is something incredibly powerful that happens in your brain. It creates this marvelous connection, a rewiring of your nervous system that redefines you in a way that doing something once or twice a week will never accomplish. When you create this unbroken continuum of activity, your brain decides that's part of who you are now, your new self-definition.

You can see how this cuts both ways. If you play guitar every day, you're a musician. And your brain knows it. If you exercise every day, or read an hour a day, your brain knows it. If you smoke a pack a day, you're a smoker, and if you gamble every chance you get, you're a compulsive gambler. Your brain knows that and accepts it without judgment and programs it accordingly.

But if you work out once every other weekend, or pick up your guitar whenever you feel like it, then your brain knows that too. It says, "That's not who we *are*; it's just what we do occasionally." That's a huge difference. You can have good habits or bad habits, and the brain will do your bidding either way. What you do every day matters. Because being a dabbler doesn't get support from the brain. It gets resistance. The brain wants a routine.

Your brain knows whether you're a doer or a dabbler, and it reacts accordingly.

Let's go even more basic. Do you have to force yourself to brush your teeth in the morning? Hopefully not. You just do it. It's not a decision you have to make every day. Because of it, you are likely to keep your teeth a lot longer. If, for some reason, your personal hygiene is so poor that you don't brush your teeth every day, you've got the decay to show for it.

It's the same with your goals and dreams. If you don't find a way to get to them every day, even for two minutes, they will start to decay.

The human brain is lazy. It's an energy conserver. Decisions take energy. The brain is always looking to minimize the workload, so when you do something every day, the brain eliminates the decision-making process. It just goes along with the program, and it takes very little energy to get started.

Beyond reprogramming your brain, Every Day Action also works for two other reasons. First, you are adding something, no matter how small, to what you want to achieve, every single day. You're moving down the field toward your goal, even if it's only an inch closer. It aggregates continuously, and suddenly a year goes by and you've made significant progress. On the other hand, if you don't start, before you know it that whole year goes by and nothing's happened. And you are older and more discouraged about your ability to achieve your goal.

Second, committing to Every Day Action also tricks you into getting started on something. Especially if you do it early in the day. If you decide to talk to one stranger every day, and you do it in the morning while in line at your coffee place, or at work, or just standing at a red light, something magical happens. If you have some success, you realize you didn't die, and then you'll probably do it again, maybe even two more times that day. Then before you know it, you've built up this rejection/embarrassment callus because you've done the exercises consistently.

When you don't do the activity every day, then something else happens. You have to restart yourself every time, and it drifts into doing it less and less, or not doing it at all. I want to drive this point home:

We let our dreams decay because of what we DON'T do every single day to reach them.

Nothing is more fatal to a dream than the fantasy that you can get to it tomorrow, or next year, or when you have enough time or enough money or enough energy. Boldness empowers you to start now, today, and move an inch or two, and then maybe a mile. The fact is, it doesn't matter how far you go, not nearly as much as it matters how often. I will say that again: *it doesn't matter how far you go, not nearly as much as it matters how often you get to it*. Before you know it, the dream becomes real.

NEUROSCIENCE:
WHY THE PRIDE METHOD WORKS

There has been a significant amount of research done in the past ten years on the science of brain activity. For example, it was generally believed that the brain stopped developing by the time we reached twenty years old. Remarkably, it has now been proven that the brain can grow, evolve, and develop new neural pathways at any age.

Even more exciting to me is the discovery that if you change your behavior, you not only develop new neural pathways, but the more you repeat the new behavior, the more dominant the new neural pathways become. Just as important is that your old neural pathways *weaken*!

Think about the significance of that. What this means is as you act with more boldness, your brain learns this is how you are going to act in situations, and it gradually turns less and less to the hesitant behavior that you previously programmed in.

This is why the PRIDE Method works. It taps into how the brain learns and adapts to change. For decades—centuries, even—behavior modification has been attempted in different ways with mixed results, and very often with no results at all. But when you align your practice of change with how the brain functions, it happens faster and becomes permanent. In other words, you truly can change yourself neurologically and rewrite your operating system.

Think of it like a river that has been rerouted. As the river surges in the new direction, growing ever wider with the new steady flow, the old riverbed slowly dries up. This is what's happening with your neural pathways as you do the exercises.

I find this incredibly exciting because it's not theory or advice anymore. It's working with your supercomputer brain the way it wants to work, accelerating and enhancing the results. The Boldness Exercises you will do are all designed to push you in new directions, creating new neural pathways and reinforcing bold behavior until it essentially becomes natural.

This is what happened naturally with extroverts, who we see behave with boldness as part of their "personality." They created neural pathways reinforced by the success of their boldness that caused them to react to situations the opposite way that shy people do. Their reflex is to act and react with boldness. The shy neural pathway doesn't exist for them in their brains.

The research also seems to indicate that this is in part why acting happy and smiling a lot makes you feel happier. Happiness pathways are being formed in the brain, and the gloomy negative ones slowly atrophy. In other words, acting happy can make you happy. Kind of wonderful and the opposite of what most people assume. Most people are waiting for a reason to be happy. The brain is just waiting for you to decide to act that way, and it will do the rest. Kind of amazing, don't you think?

WHERE YOU WILL GET TO

These are some examples of who you can become. You may want to be all of them, some of them, or just one of them. It's up to you.

The person who volunteers first.

The person who raises her hand with a question, an opinion, or to accept a dare.

The person everyone admires because you do what they're all afraid to.

The person who offers help to strangers.

The person who meets whoever she wants to meet, whatever the situation, and however important or famous or aloof they may be.

The person who doesn't take the safe seat with people he already knows, but plunks down between two new people.

The person who steps up and defends someone while everyone else waits to see who else will speak up.

The person who delivers the heartfelt eulogy, memorable toast, or brilliant presentation.

You can do all this while still being the real you. The new, improved, fully revealed and realized you.

CHAPTER 5

PREPARATION

There are two stages to Preparation in the PRIDE Method. The first includes general behavior guidelines, tips, and techniques that ground you in social situations. I find that many people don't know these (I didn't, for a long time). Some of them are shifts in mindset, and others are simply alterations in behavior. Because there are so many of these, I've tackled them separately in Part III, "Foundations." In that part, we'll cover the Guiding Principles, Social Skills, and Power Tools that will help you in your social interactions.

The second stage is Preparation for specific actions, starting with the Boldness Exercises then, of course, carrying them into your daily life as you progress into boldness. Think of this second stage of Preparation as the specific things you need to do mentally, right before you take action. This is what we'll cover in this chapter.

WHY PREPARE?

When it comes to social skills, I often hear people say, "Why should I have to learn how to act around people? It should come naturally; otherwise, it just seems fake or rehearsed."

This is just your self-defeating voice, Doctor No, kicking in. Ignore it. We generally don't believe we need to prepare for social interactions. How absurd is that? We prepare for driving tests, football tryouts, bar exams, bar mitzvahs, job interviews, and yet, for what we do most—day-to-day interactions with people—most of us just go blindly and unprepared into every encounter. Why should we automatically know what to say and how to act in every situation? It's misguided at best.

Humans don't have instincts for our behavior like animals do. It's almost all learned. Most of us are stuck with our parents' way of interacting with people, and there are a whole lot of parents out there with a limited range of social skills. That's not counting the parents with morality issues, psychological problems, and general bad manners. They're not preparing their kids to interact well with the world. And very few of them are preparing them to act with confidence and boldness.

Maybe you didn't have very social parents. Or maybe they just didn't know that much about raising confident children. Or maybe they were very bold naturally and you weren't, and so you went in the other direction. No matter what, they most likely did not have a *systematic* way for you to overcome your shyness and build self-confidence.

"Don't be shy," would be a common parent's admonishment to their child. OK, where's the switch I flip off so that I'm not shy anymore? I sure didn't have that switch. I had an amplifier knob that seemed to turn in only one direction. As soon as they said, "Don't be shy," my shyness bumped up several notches because now I was *aware* that people were noticing my bashful behavior, and I really withdrew. Preparation is the first step in actively changing your reaction and strengthening you to venture into your discomfort zone.

What follows are three specific behavioral tools that will help you build confidence before you venture into boldness. Remember, there's a lot more coming in Part III, *and* we'll be breaking down the specific types of Preparation you need before each Boldness Exercise in Part IV. So don't worry—you'll have many tools in your arsenal before you venture into the world. I've got you.

EXPECT REJECTION, REDEFINE FAILURE

Perhaps the most important step in Preparation is this: learn to expect rejection. In fact, you'll be deliberately seeking it in some of the Boldness Exercises. It's important to know and accept this very simple fact: not everyone will find you interesting. This doesn't make you a freak; it makes you normal. *No one* is interesting to everyone. I guarantee you that some people would have no interest in meeting Justin Timberlake, or Taylor Swift, or Tom Hanks, or even Abraham Lincoln. Prepare yourself for this and it will not hurt. At least not for long.

In short, learn to reject rejection. Which is a lot easier when you redefine it.

We interpret rejection as some sort of failure. But when we let go of failure as a fear and make it a goal, then rejection falls by the wayside. One of the most transformational stages of learning boldness is learning to accept that you will inherently not be good at some things at the outset. In other words, you will experience failure—at least, that's what you used to call it. It's time to start calling it "learning."

That's what Dosage is about and why Preparation is important. The trick is to make the failures simply steps upward, stages of learning and growing, not something any more painful than a hard workout or a well-executed sales pitch where you didn't close the deal. You gave it your best shot and have something to mine for some lessons. That's not something to be afraid of. But because it's social, I know it carries more juice. So, we're going to nibble at it and make the transition little by little.

Once you get beyond that fear of failure, you will start to embrace it, revel in it, and enjoy it, because it means you are on the path. The beginning of most learning is the most painful part and usually the most discouraging.

You have a choice. You can say, "I'm terrible at this. I hate this. I wish it were easier!" Or you can say, "I'm terrible at this, which means I'm at the very exciting part, the very beginning of learning something new. And because it's so hard, it will be a great challenge and be incredibly satisfying when I get good at it."

Which choice are you going to make?

For example, you will meet people at a party whose attention always seems elsewhere, like they are looking for something or someone better than you at that moment. In fact, that's exactly what they are doing, and they are always doing it. It's their behavior in most situations. So, expect it to happen. It is not a reflection on you.

Even if it were, why care? Why would anyone's opinion besides your own matter? Or at the very least, why would it matter *more* than your own? I know right now it matters—even pains you—to feel rejection. But this nonchalance about others' opinions is a powerful new mindset that you're going to get to, a little at a time.

Journal Entry #5: Ranking Other People's Opinions

Let's pause for a moment to explore this new mindset through a journal entry. How do you start to care less about other people's opinions? The first step is to change the *weight* of other people's opinions. They should matter, at least a tiny bit, let's face it. Otherwise, you're a bit of a sociopath. But it has to be in balance with how important they are in your life. Your boss's opinion matters a lot. Perhaps as much as your own, when it comes to your work performance.

Now, on a scale of 1 to 10, let's lay out how much specific people's opinions about you should matter (you can put in your own number—these are mine):

Your spouse/partner: 8 (It should matter almost as much as yours, but not replace it.)

Mentors: 10 (If your mentor's opinion doesn't matter as much as your own, why are they your mentor?)

Close friends: 8

Facebook "friends": 1

Coworkers: 4

Audience members: 5

Random strangers: 0

You can be more specific with this list and use actual names as well. The point is to give yourself a realistic perspective on what weight you're giving to their opinions.

Add to this list in your journal, with rankings, along with the names of people in your life and how you honestly believe you should rank them.

You're going to find out as you move up the scale toward superboldness that there are people more socially inept than you once were. You are suddenly going to be on the other side of the fence, and the closet-case shy people are going to be judging you, rejecting you, ignoring you, and even insulting you. (You know, maybe like you used to do.) This is a good sign, because everything they do is a reflection of the state they are in and how unhappy they are with it. It is NOT a reflection on you, so why would you care about someone's opinion who is trapped where you no longer are?

Let me tell you an interesting incident that happened recently. There is a place near my office where people jaywalk all the time, and one day there was a policeman lying in wait for anyone who attempted it. A woman was about to cross, saw the officer, and instead walked around to the crossing light where I was also waiting. I looked at her and said, "I'm surprised. They really are writing jaywalking tickets. They never do."

Instead of responding, she turned and looked away, and at the same time did a little dismissive flick of her wrist in my direction. It shocked me. It was like I had asked her for spare change. But then I laughed to myself. "What an amazing total fail," I thought. I was so unobtrusively friendly, and she was so exceptionally rude to me that I almost said, "I'm sorry, I didn't realize you were too special to talk to."

But I didn't say anything equally rude like that, and I'm glad, because there is nothing to be gained by that, and I would just be showing that this insignificant encounter somehow could affect me disproportionately. Instead, I imagined that whatever headspace she was in, or whatever social skill level she was at, I simply chose the wrong moment to speak to her. Nothing more. Nothing to worry about or retreat into shyness about. Just the opposite. A perfect example of how you will not always connect, no matter how at ease you become.

My brother told me an even crazier story. He was walking down the street in Santa Monica, a true bicycle-rider's mecca, and as he stood on the sidewalk a woman on a bike came to a stop in front of him, and he smiled at her. With all the vitriol she could muster, she shouted, "F*ck you!" to him. All he had done was smile at her. He didn't even say hi and she went antisocially ballistic. Who knows what headspace she was in to respond with such hostility to a stranger smiling at her?

The point of these stories is the same: you can NEVER know where people's lives and heads are at, so don't worry about it when they react bizarrely. It's not you, and even if it is you, so what? Move on. Leave it where it belongs, in the past.

Think about all the times you were embarrassed by doing something that drew attention to yourself. What made it bad was your reaction to it, to choose to feel embarrassed. None of us is perfect, and no one expects us to be perfect, nor do we expect other people to be. Yet we want to be, and we're embarrassed when we aren't, unaware that it is a choice to feel that way.

Imagine a scenario where you are in a restaurant and you spill something on the table, or worse, knock a glass onto the floor and it breaks. It *could* be embarrassing. It doesn't *have* to be. You can choose to stand up and say, "And for my next trick..." or "Show's over, folks. Next performance at ten o'clock." Hard to do? Not really. Why should it be? Only because you tell yourself it is. It's not hard to stand up and say words. People do it all the time. You could too.

But you've added this extra charge to it, this definition of what is acceptable, appropriate, or not showing off, or a dozen other self-imposed excuses for why that's a response choice you would never make (Remember "Nature, Nurture, and Conforming" in Chapter 3?). But is it difficult? Not at all. Physically, it's ridiculously easy. Which is why the psychology of it is so fascinating. Our minds, our twisted, inhibited, over-thinking brains, can stop our bodies from the most effortless of actions.

This is an example of the process of *redefinition*. This will be part of your Preparation. You will redefine actions that scare you as something harmless. In the Boldness Exercises, you will simplify and redefine what you're doing. In one of the exercises, I have you walking into the stock room of a supermarket. But in your mind, you are not walking into the back room of a grocery store. You are simply walking forward twenty steps. That's it.

You will be speaking to many individuals in these exercises. But you are not doing the dreaded talking to a stranger. You are simply saying words out loud while looking at someone. Eventually you will redefine speaking to a roomful of people as not public speaking, but simply speaking. Because that's all it is.

If the definition is holding you back, redefine it as part of your Preparation. This re-definition will change your state of mind if you just let it. In so doing, you've changed the weight of the action in your mind by reducing it to a harmless meaning.

This is nothing short of a change in your worldview. We have a tendency to overload things with excess meaning, often a meaning that causes us to hesitate or misjudge the situation completely. If a definition is holding you back, redefine it. Trim off the excess baggage and put it in its simplest form. Then action becomes easier.

Each moment of boldness amounts to you stepping forward, showing up, letting the next thing happen, bearing the consequences, and labeling them as learning, positive, and worthwhile.

This is a big leap, going from fearing rejection to expecting it. Some of the Boldness Exercises will even have you inviting it. Sounds like fun, doesn't it? It will be.

YOUR THEME SONG

I want to give you a secret weapon in preparing yourself for bold actions and interactions. It's your theme song. Think of it just like a soundtrack, creating a specific emotion in yourself, amplifying your confidence, and juicing up your self-image. It will be a great enhancement to your Boldness Exercises. It's something you choose for yourself, a song that motivates you, drives you, excites you, and gives you energy and confidence. We're not talking some sappy ballad here. We want "Roar" or "Eye of the Tiger"-level stuff.

I personally like "Uptown Funk" by Bruno Mars. Your song should be something that if you were alone, you couldn't resist dancing to with a big smile on your face. Take the time to seek out this song. Make sure you have it on your phone in case you need to remind yourself. You could even make it your ringtone.

Your songs can change over time. You may start with Taylor Swift's "Shake It Off" (when you're trying to turn rejection into learning) and then evolve to something by Drake or The Who. You can have different theme songs for different situations.

The idea is to play the theme song in your head (or maybe in your headphones, to start) as part of your Preparation for a Boldness Exercise. That way, before you approach someone, or walk into a party, or a meeting, or an interview, you're using it to enhance your mental and physical state.

Great moments, bold moments, deserve a soundtrack. You will eventually have a repertoire of songs that you play in your head, depending on the situation. But for now, find one.

SUMMON CONFIDENCE FROM
YOUR MEMORIES

In Chapter 1, you listed your Moments That Made a Difference in your journal: those moments where you acted boldly or with confidence. You are going to use these to summon confidence in new situations. You are going to replay the memory of those specific incidents to find strength by putting yourself back in that place.

You will actually close your eyes and think about that time, that occasion when you said exactly what you wanted to say, or did exactly what you wanted to do, and how good that felt. Then open your eyes and carry that feeling forward into the new situation.

This is a very powerful tool. You are transferring confidence from one experience to another. The principle is simple: you had confidence in a specific situation. So why not take it with you everywhere? The only difference is the circumstance, which you are currently letting diminish your confidence. Reverse that and wear your confidence like a superhero costume that you can slip into at a moment's notice.

Practice this before the exercises, as well as with other situations in your life. You'll discover that it will fill your body with the same positive chemicals and alter your state in the direction of boldness.

CHAPTER 6

RELAXING AND INSIGHT

n this chapter, we'll cover two stages of the PRIDE Method: Relaxing and Insight.

RELAXING

Nervousness is a remarkable thing, physiologically speaking. First of all, what's with the armpits? And the forehead? What is with the overworking cooling system? Clearly the body is anticipating some extreme danger that it imagines is real and feels compelled to run the air-conditioning. Then it also jams up our memory, ties our tongue, and generally turns us into a social cripple. How helpful.

Being relaxed, on the other hand, is also remarkable. It is amazing what we can think of to say if we just stay calm. We are articulate, clever even. We remember things, and our body doesn't exhibit excess fluids. Words come out in the right order.

To many people, there are some situations where being relaxed seems impossible. It isn't. There are a number of things you can do to change your state of anxiety. I'm not saying it will be eliminated, but it will be under control. And that's a big difference. Eventually that tension you feel will become energy that you tap into, but at the beginning, we are just going to reduce that nervous, sweaty, brain-damaged state you find yourself in into something manageable.

Of course, the main reason you should want to achieve this transformation, beyond just not appearing nervous, is that when we are not relaxed, we tend to be incoherent. This is different than being a little tongue-tied. This is tongue-twisted and brain-twisted combined. We tend to babble and bobble our thoughts, overeager to speak but not mentally stable enough, so we garble the transmission from brain to tongue.

Everything you do in the PRIDE Method will change that.

I'm sure you've noticed that nervousness and shyness combine to reduce your access to your memory. It happens to everyone who isn't in a relaxed state. Untrained actors forget their lines—the same lines they memorized and could repeat practically in their sleep—when they get onstage and suddenly get anxious. They forget one or two words, then their brain registers the mistake, amps up the anxiety, and suddenly the whole line or the whole speech is gone. Where did it go? Behind the anxiety curtain.

The more you do the Boldness Exercises and apply the Relaxing techniques, the more you'll also cure your memory loss.

Nervousness and anxiety spiral upward if we don't know how to relax. When we do start to relax, they start to spiral downward, and you're back in control.

So, it seems important to find a way to relax in those moments when we feel anxious. First of all, it seldom helps to radiate nervousness. When we're anxious, people sense it and often it makes them anxious. Many situations in life are not just an encounter, but a performance. Meeting someone new, applying for a job, or giving a speech all require the appearance of confidence and poise.

Note that I said "appearance." This is what you need to realize: many actors can be nervous the entire time they are onstage or on camera, but the good ones never appear that way. The trick is to take that fear reaction and turn it into positive energy, fuel for a performance. "Wait, how will that happen, exactly?" you ask skeptically.

NOT by someone telling you to relax. I'm sure you know that doesn't work. That is, unless you have a technique for doing it.

Preparation is the first step to reducing that anxiety. There is a lot less pressure when you are prepared. You know what you're going to say or do. You already expect rejection and have redefined failure into learning. You're tapping into your confident memories, and you're playing your theme song. Then the step following Relaxing, Step 3, Insight, will also help to relax you. Remember, the PRIDE Method is a matrix. Each element reinforces the other.

So now we're going to add two powerful techniques to bring you into a state of greater relaxation: breathing and physiology.

Breathing

Breathing has a remarkable effect. It is one of the simplest and most powerful ways to relax yourself.

You can calm yourself down several degrees just by taking a short series of deep breaths. The few times I still get nervous walking onstage, that is what I do. I shake my body to loosen up, lower my shoulders, and take a few long, slow breaths.

You may still be nervous, but less so. The fact that you are more relaxed starts to move you in the right direction. Instead of your anxiety spiraling upward, you've dialed it back and realized that you can. Big step.

Remember, one of the crazy things we do when we are nervous or anxious is hold our breath. Oxygen is vital to consciousness. Give yourself some extra, rather than less, and it will do wonders.

Try it. Do it with your eyes closed, right now. Take three long, slow, deep breaths. No matter what state you happen to be in, you will start to feel more relaxed.

What you will discover is that once you do become more relaxed, you can think more clearly, you can remember to smile, make eye contact, you can kill your hesitation, and you can take that first bold step.

Doing the Boldness Exercises will make it so you can relax, in part, because of Step 4, Dosage control. You're going to progress gradually out of your comfort zone, and you're not going to overwhelm yourself as you advance in your confidence and boldness. All the PRIDE steps work in balance to progress you gradually and steadily forward.

An even more powerful method for using breath to relax yourself is called the Vagus Breath Technique. The vagus nerves are a pair of nerves that run down through the heart and lungs into the digestive tract. There is a way of vibrating the vagus nerve that will relax you quite nicely. This is also called "diaphragmatic breathing"—breathing from your diaphragm. Eastern yogis have known about it for centuries, but in recent years, scientific research has shown that the Vagus Breath Technique can actually reduce the fight-or-flight reaction.

So here's how to do it:

1. Close your eyes.
2. Inhale deeply through your nose, filling your lungs as much as possible.
3. Exhale slowly through your mouth, making a low "Aaaahhh" sound as you do it.
4. Repeat two or three more times.

If you're in a public place, instead of making a sound, you can simply exhale slowly through your mouth, holding your lips together like you're blowing out a whole lot of birthday candles.

Breathing is intensely effective, and most people do it worst when they need it the most. Employ it with all your Boldness Exercises (and in real life too!) along with the other PRIDE Method steps, and you will radically relax yourself, especially if you do the second technique: adjusting your physiology.

Adjusting Your Physiology

You can move into a more relaxed state simply by focusing on your physiology—your body position—and changing it.

Anytime you find yourself moving into your discomfort zone, notice your body position and posture, especially before and during the Boldness Exercises. Did you suddenly fold your arms tightly in front of you? Are you talking sideways to the person rather than head on? Are your hands in your pockets? Crossed in front of your privates? Are you slouching? Are you looking down? Are you not smiling?

Develop the habit of running a routine check on your body position and where you might be holding tension. It's very easy to become detached from our nervous reactions and how we physicalize them. Watch for these:

- Clenching your teeth
- Frowning
- Folding your arms tightly in front of you
- Pushing your shoulders up around your neck
- Pushing your bottom lip out
- Pursing your lips
- Clenching your fists
- Holding your breath
- Tightening your stomach
- Hunching forward
- Drooping your shoulders
- Looking down or away
- Locking your knees

Along with breath exercises, adjusting your body is essential to releasing tension. It won't be easy at first, and you'll be surprised when you start catching yourself. You'll find yourself asking, "What are my shoulders doing up so high?" or "Why am I looking at my feet?" Nervousness makes us do strange things unconsciously, but they reflect our internal condition.

You will need to develop body adjustments that relax you from head to toe. Eventually you won't need to be this methodical, as you will be able to quickly make the physical adjustments as soon as you catch yourself tensing up. But for now, follow these body adjustment steps:

1. Shake your body out by twisting from the waist with your arms hanging loosely.
2. Turn your head from left to right a few times.
3. Shake your arms and hands.
4. Drop your shoulders (if they are up around your neck).
5. Straighten up—shoulders back, head erect, spine straight.
6. Stretch your face with an exaggerated smile.
7. Say something out loud. This will clear your throat and get you to a good volume level. Usually just one word, like "Yes," but say it fairly loudly. Pretend you are talking on your phone if people are around.

You're ready for action. That is, as soon as you realize and accept a few important insights.

INSIGHT

Part of what will move you from shyness to boldness are insights into what bold individuals already know about life, about human nature, and about opportunities. This whole book really is about insights that will change your mindset, but I want to go into more detail on the essential ones that I listed earlier.

Insight #1

People are not thinking about you as much as you think they are.

The first key Insight about shyness and embarrassment comes down to this very powerful realization that people are just not thinking about you that much.

That is the simple fact—they are spending very little time thinking about you. They are thinking about themselves and, ironically, about what other people might be thinking about *them*. It's the great contradiction in our behavior. People may laugh at you, or tell a story about you, or have a judgment, but they are going to forget about it quickly and return to their own self-absorption. This may leave you feeling embarrassed or rejected if you choose to experience it that way. But embedded in this Insight is an essential fact: *how you experience these things is a choice.*

As you start to expect rejection and redefine it, this Insight makes it that much easier. Don't assume their rejection has some vast, deeper meaning.

I know you worry about what other people think. And yes, people will gossip. They will have judgments. Do you think they need factual information to do this? Do you think they are even *interested* in the facts? Why would that be interesting? Most of the time, it certainly isn't.

Conjecture and supposition hold boundless rewards to the gossiper, compared to the truth. Bold people, on the other hand, could care less about gossip, even if it is about them. They're too busy enjoying their lives.

Most people believe their own expectations and biases about people. They have a natural tendency to believe the worst about people they don't like and the best about people they do. Political beliefs are the extreme example of this. Everyone in their political party has the best ideas and the best intentions, and everyone in the other party is a crook, a liar, and an idiot. It's called the *horns/halo effect*. These beliefs almost never reflect reality or the truth. I'm telling you this so you'll have the Insight that *what people think about you is totally out of your control.* Stop focusing on it.

This is the perspective you have to have: if someone has a judgment about you from an embarrassing moment, so what? The reality is that no one has lived flawlessly cool lives. More likely they are riddled with their own insecurities. (Which is why they want to judge you—it makes them feel better about themselves.) So, it doesn't matter. The rest of the people didn't notice, care, or love you and don't have a judgment about you. But either way, the equation is imbalanced. You're giving too much weight to the wrong side, and you're the only one paying any sort of price, when there is no toll due. Stop paying. Ride for free. That's what bold people do.

Use this Insight to stop doing what most people do, which is worry about what other people think. Release yourself from that imaginary bondage.

Insight #2

In reality, you are almost never in real danger.

The second and equally important Insight is the simple fact that 99 percent of the time, you are in no real danger. But your body is reacting as if it is. We have evolved into a species that has replaced our response to nonlethal threats with a lethal fear reaction. It's bizarre, unproductive, and unnecessary. To break out of your prison, you must accurately assess what is truly dangerous and what is imaginary.

Our brain is a remarkable thing. It has the ability to conjure up the sensation of pain when there is no actual injury. Don't believe me? Have you ever been up in a high observation tower like the one in Toronto, where they have a plexiglass section of the floor that allows you to look straight down one thousand feet? For most people, as they do it, a bolt of lightning shoots up their butt. It's perfectly safe, but the brain is pretty sure you're about to die and sounds the alarm.

This is what we do with emotional situations. We generate actual pain, or at least intense discomfort. And that reaction doesn't just cause pain; it impairs you. Walk on a balance beam on the ground, and you will most likely not fall off until you get twenty feet or farther. Walk on one three feet up, and most people won't get three steps. Why? Fear impairs us.

This is what you do with your social fears. Your brain takes over and creates a sensation of genuine injury where there is none. It manifests real pain just by the thought of something. How marvelous. This is why dread and apprehension make us sweat under our arms. It's not warmer in the room—your brain has just decided there's danger and is starting its emergency sprinkler system. Some of us even stop breathing. How is that helpful? But in our primitive self, part of concealment from danger was not breathing, I guess. So that's our reaction. Being tongue-tied is your brain telling you it's safer *not* to speak. Now that's some false messaging there.

Can you also see how counterproductive it is, how inhibiting?

In short, you have to learn to become fearless of the harmless.

In most situations where you are feeling hesitant, paralyzed, or fearful, nothing bad will actually occur. Certainly nothing life-threatening. The rest is your imagination making movies of the worst scenarios and causing you to feel genuine pain. Your body may be reacting as if the danger is real, but nothing physically harmful is going to happen to you. You need to realize this: *no one has ever actually died of embarrassment*. It doesn't feel good, and we of course have this terrible fear of being ostracized by the tribe. But you actually control these things more than you think.

Let's talk a bit more about this tribe thing. The reason most of us respond so strongly to rejection is that deep inside our lizard brain, there is this programming that kept us alive on the African plains once we started walking upright a million or so years ago. One of the most critical motivations was to continue to be accepted by the tribe. (This is still true with many primates today, by the way—just watch Animal Planet and you'll see.)

Back then, being rejected by the tribe meant you were probably going to die fairly quickly. No other tribe was likely to accept you, and they'd probably just kill you. So we became highly attuned to whenever the tribe was not responding positively to us, with an alarm of imminent danger. It was essential to fit in. And somehow this is still true in high school today, even after a million years of evolution, because our brains haven't evolved as fast as society has.

Thus, we feel real danger, a real threat to our existence, when we experience rejection. Therefore, this Insight is absolutely essential that we are having a confused, faulty, and primitive reaction that doesn't serve us in the modern world, and that reaction will only disappear when we venture beyond it.

This Insight comes from a rational thought process where you are realistic about the true repercussions of your actions. This is a calculation I'm going to insist you keep making. **What is the *real* downside, and what is the *real* upside to the specific action?**

Most of the time, our fears create a disproportionately huge and fictional downside, and our lack of social experience with adventurous, bold behavior doesn't allow us to accurately calculate the potential upside. I'll say it more simply: your fears create a bleak scenario that is purely fiction.

If you're not building nuclear power plants or a spaceship to Mars, then you don't need to focus on the worst-case scenario. Give it a rest.

Insight #3

It's time to start listening to Doctor Yes.

The third Insight is based on the fact that the negative voice in your head is wrong. Even if Doctor No's warnings have been right sometimes, who cares? They're wrong so much more often that it's worthless information, so stop its influence on you. You wouldn't watch a news station that was wrong 95 percent of the time, would you? Remember the axiom: don't believe everything you think. It's time to give voice to Doctor Yes. Give yourself the Insight of the positive possibilities.

Doctor Yes is all about the upside, and you need to start cultivating this voice. Tell yourself the greatest possible outcome. And maybe the greatest outcome is you made the effort and you feel great no matter what the outcome.

Doctor Yes finds the win in everything. Doctor Yes is optimistic that even if this isn't a win right now, it's a step toward a bigger win. Think of that salesperson who gets hung up on a cold call, and says, "Thank you!" because she knows that she's one more call closer to her next sale.

There is now scientific research that supports this. It's been demonstrated that when people tell themselves something isn't possible, or it's too hard, then the brain basically steps off the task and doesn't do the creative work necessary. But if the brain hears that we believe it's possible, it steps up and starts looking for ways to make it happen.

All of us need a little brainwashing. Washing our brain of the pollution of negativity requires pumping in fresh, clean, positive ideas. This process of giving Doctor Yes a voice "rinses out" the negative thoughts.

Start listening to Doctor Yes, and it will release you from the grip of negativity and give you the motivation to act.

Here's more food for thought. It's not about getting to that place where you are completely comfortable all the time. Because the real goal is to be both relaxed and uncomfortable at the same time. Sounds kind of impossible, but you will eventually create moments when it happens. You will certainly want to be *more* comfortable, and not so nervous you can't act or speak, but you'll want to be walking to the edge of your comfort zone and stepping over it while hanging onto as much of that relaxed state as possible. Relaxed and uncomfortable. That's where the discovery is.

Insight #4

You need to give yourself permission to have the life you want.

The final and perhaps most powerful Insight is that all that is required for you to have the life you want is to give yourself permission to do so.

You've heard my story in Chapter 2, so you know I learned this the hard way. Believe me when I tell you: you are the one who is withholding that permission. The. Only. One.

This may seem absurd to you right now. You are certain that there are many outside forces that control the outcome of your daily life, and many things in your past that have kept you from just deciding to alter your behavior and change your life.

Wait. Doesn't behavior modification take years of therapy? And even then, who really changes? Almost all of us, is the reality. But most of us change for the worse because we give up on our dreams. I'll say that again: we all change, but most of us change because we *gave up* on our dreams, not because we failed to reach them. And because we never gave ourselves permission to simply start living the life we wanted, regardless of the consequences. The worst consequence of all is dying and not having lived the life you wanted to.

Let this thought guide you until you have enough discoveries to know that this is the truth: many of the most wonderful memories of your life— the turning points, the epiphanies, the overwhelming joys—happened when you stepped outside your comfort zone. *And they only could have happened because you crossed that line.*

Burn these four insights into your mindset and watch what happens.

CHAPTER 7

DOSAGE

O n the path to boldness, controlling the intensity of any experience is essential to maximize the result without overwhelming ourselves. We don't want to underdose and be ineffective, and we don't want to overdose and become paralyzed or traumatized. This is why the Boldness Exercises in Part IV are divided into levels: they're designed to vaccinate you against the stress of being bolder by limiting the intensity of the experience to something you can tolerate.

In medicine, an inoculation is an exposure to a mild form of the disease to build up your resistance. Same here, except we're talking about your discomfort zone. What is also important to remember is that your personal Dosage is not the same as everyone else's.

The principle of Dosage extends beyond the vaccine concept to another pharmaceutical analogy. With drugs, when you increase your dosage, you gradually build up a tolerance. Similarly, when you increase the challenges to your lack of confidence gradually enough, you will also develop a tolerance —and you'll become addicted to boldness!

You will hear me talk a lot about your *discomfort zone*. I'll remind you that this is any activity outside your comfort zone. Everyone's discomfort zone is different, and the further you go into it, the more intensely you will feel uncomfortable, with your false danger sensors going off louder and louder.

With the Boldness Exercises, I want you to feel a certain level of discomfort, and I expect you to be willing to increase that as you feel stronger and more confident. Only you can decide what you can handle. But don't be too gentle with yourself, or it will be like trying to get in shape by doing one push-up a day.

Stress will make you stronger, just like it does in exercise. You can get as far as you want if you pace yourself and stick with the exercises. But it's also about stressing yourself to the edge of your tolerable level. Otherwise, you're not building your social muscles.

Remember, everyone's tolerance is different. Once you understand this aspect of Dosage—that everyone is different—it should be easier to stop comparing your social abilities to those of other people. Some people can sing beautifully a cappella standing on a street corner, and other people are comfortable panhandling on that same corner. Other people can't even raise their voice in an argument, or hail a taxi, never mind sing in public. Whatever got us this way—which in the end is not important, only fixing it is—*our Dosage is our Dosage*, and what other people can handle is irrelevant.

Also, the level where you start to build your tolerance will be your own. You may race through the first level of the Boldness Exercises, or you could spend two weeks working just on nonverbal communication like a big smile to someone or a nod. It doesn't matter. Start at whatever level your nervous system can handle. You are simply discovering the boundaries of your personal discomfort zone. Don't worry; where you start does not determine how far you'll get. You determine that. It's up to you.

Dosage is also a strategy of controlling the intensity of the failure. First of all, with most of the Boldness Exercises, the goal is failure. But it can't be too drastic, too intense, or you will bail on me. I want you in your discomfort zone, but not so far that you can't see your way back home. Survivable failures are the key, just as it is with most of life, whether it be in business, investment, science, or relationships. It's all about Dosage, my bold ones!

THE PROPER DOSAGE LEVEL

The Boldness Exercises are designed to be progressive in Dosage intensity, allowing you to build your tolerance.

We all experience a certain level of what I call "new encounter anxiety." For some of us, it is intense and others mild. But it's perfectly natural. We all have a desire to be accepted. This can get amplified when it's someone we really want to meet. Which is why in the Boldness Exercises we will practice on people where the encounter is insignificant so that the failure has little to no impact on your psyche.

You want to be prepared—there's that word again—by practicing with lower-intensity encounters so you don't freeze when you encounter a person you'd really like to meet, whether it's a celebrity, a stranger who can give you directions, or a doorman who can let you into a club. Or the future love of your life.

Lowering the risk to something insignificant is a Dosage trick that helps you relax and build your confidence muscles. The Roman philosopher Seneca would wear a purple toga—not a popular color back then—to deliberately do something embarrassing but unimportant, so as to vaccinate himself against embarrassment. That's why the exercises will include embarrassing yourself doing trivial things—wearing a funny hat, leaving your fly down, putting some lipstick on your teeth—things that (hopefully) won't do any psychological damage.

Just like you would practice your backhand in tennis or your three-point shot in basketball so you can react quickly in a real game, you need to practice when there is very little at stake. The point of the early exercises in particular is to give you the experience of an encounter without the risk. You want to create a series of nice little satisfying successes and harmless failures.

Understand that you can push yourself to a point of social fatigue. You've only got so much jam to pursue these challenges in any given session. Dosage is also about how long the venture is into your discomfort zone, as well as how intense the challenge is.

Finally, these early successes will lend truth to the four key insights. You will start to realize that they are actually true, unlike what you've been telling yourself all your life. And that will reinforce your determination, encourage you to increase your Dosage, and accelerate your pathway to boldness.

Let me continue the analogy to physical exercise. Just as you can push too hard and injure yourself and not be able to work out for months, you can overstress yourself trying to be bolder before you're strong enough. Conversely, if you are too easy on yourself in every workout, you won't get any stronger. Same with confidence-building. You have to break a sweat in both.

Let me give you another sports analogy. After falling hopelessly behind in the first half of Super Bowl LI, New England Patriots' quarterback Tom Brady won the game by doing one simple thing: focusing on the next ten yards. He didn't throw a series of Hail Mary passes in the hope that he might get lucky. He knew that if he advanced ten more yards, he would get one more chance to go ten more yards, until he scored a touchdown. And then he scored again the same way. That's how you need to work. Focus on the gain of the exercise, not leaping forward ten steps. And every once in a while, just as it did with Brady in that game, the breakthroughs happen.

Also, I recommend you do your Boldness Exercises early in the day so you can gauge how significant the stress of the situation really was. Maybe you'll do it again or try a harder exercise, increasing the Dosage.

If you notice, most people who work out regularly do it early in the day. Same principle.

The Boldness Exercises will change your behavior and responses to situations until you reach a point where the PRIDE steps are so ingrained that you do them unconsciously. For now, the way you will advance is by using the PRIDE Method through various levels of exercises, gradually advancing in the direction of true, self-embodied boldness.

Your progress will almost be like losing weight through an effective diet, where you see a pound or two a week disappearing. The difference with the PRIDE Method exercises is the weight that you will be losing are the stories that are holding you down, the hesitance and reticence that have been holding you back, dragging like anchors along the bottom of your psyche. You will actually feel lighter as your boldness grows.

WHY DOSAGE MATTERS

Afraid to Fail? Of Course!

Every day I read some new suggestion or saying online, either on Facebook, Twitter, or LinkedIn, telling people that failing is the key to growth, so don't be afraid of it. "The only real failure is failing to try," for example. Or, "It's only a failure if you don't learn from it."

But none of these motivational expressions explain *how* you defeat the grip that fear has on you. It's true that unboldness is often about the fear of failure or of being wrong or embarrassed.

Embarrassment is one of the main reasons people don't want to fail. They don't want to be seen failing, so they don't attempt anything and thus shield themselves from embarrassment. Which is why Dosage is so important.

You may have a fear of flying, but if you were to fly a hundred short flights in a year, then you simply couldn't sustain that fear. The brain just says, "This is too much work to stress about. Nothing bad ever happens." And so it shuts off the fear alarm.

You conquer most fears gradually, not in giant leaps. What we need are simple steps to make us willing to move out of our comfort zone long enough to develop a taste for something more, and an understanding that we won't die, because we controlled the intensity of the risk.

I've come to believe that shyness is almost a form of posttraumatic stress disorder, or PTSD, because usually an event or series of experiences caused your shyness, or diminished your confidence, just as traumatic experiences in soldiers can have a profound effect on them. You may not even remember the trigger events, as you were probably too young. Or perhaps you do, but being aware of them doesn't make their effects go away. The more intense those events and the more they were repeated, the more damaging they were to your confidence and the smaller your comfort zone. I'm sure there seems to be no way of reversing those effects.

The latest treatment for PTSD is a method called *prolonged-exposure therapy*, where the patients immerse themselves in the memories that traumatized them, all while being in a very safe environment, allowing them to release the stress caused by the experience gradually. In other words, diffusing the fear by reengaging it over and over, in a Dosage they can handle.

Please don't think I'm dismissing the difficulty of PTSD. It's a very challenging disorder, and the people with it—especially those who experienced it fighting for their country—deserve our complete support and compassion. I simply want to point out a therapy that has worked for some of them and the parallel to the earlier traumas and experiences that may be the root cause of your unboldness.

Also, this immersion form of therapy brings up an important point: you can't hide from these experiences. They will affect your life until you decide to face them head-on. Dosage control allows you to do that, and then allows you to retreat into your comfort zone to restore yourself for the next round.

In life, we all need a safe harbor from time to time, but we have to make sure we sail out of it to discover the world.

The Mind Creates Pain

Take a moment and picture yourself getting blood drawn by an inept phlebotomist. Most people immediately feel a cringe, a jolt of electricity running down through their butt at the thought of getting a needle jabbed into them clumsily and painfully. Interesting, isn't it? Nothing has physically happened, and yet *the thought alone* has created a physical manifestation of pain. Well, the same thing happens with embarrassment. We feel it physically.

In that sense, putting yourself out there socially is genuinely painful, especially when you don't get the response you hope for. We feel the pain just like when we imagine having a syringe jabbed into us. Let's change that. I'm going to get you thinking like a rugby player. Rugby is essentially football without any protective equipment. Getting hurt in the game is not only possible but almost guaranteed. You will feel pain. But what you find out when you play is that you are physically made for pain. This is true of a number of contact sports, from soccer to lacrosse.

The point is, we are not meant to take it easy. That's not being fully alive. Our body has all sorts of systems to deal with pain and continue what we are doing.

Unfortunately, when we create pain from social fear, our body doesn't have any coping measures, it seems, like it does with physical injury. I tore my Achilles tendon a couple of years ago and it hurt like crazy, but when I think about it now, I don't get the pain back. But someone can hurt our feelings, and ten years later we can bring the pain of that moment back like it was two minutes ago. We can be embarrassed all over again and feel like we've been punched in the gut. This is quite a psychological phenomenon. I call it a *distortion factor*. We've distorted false injury to a level where it exceeds real harm.

What the brain can do is adjust its interpretation and not create that pain. But that requires having the Insight that there's no danger (Insight #2) by exposing ourselves consistently to the "threat" and controlling the Dosage. This is the key to rewiring the brain.

This is why Dosage and Every Day Action are such important steps (and, of course, having Insight). The pain of the social encounters in the Boldness Exercises should never be so intense that you will retreat into your shell. Then we'll step it up and up and up until you don't even realize you've been boldly flying at thirty-five thousand feet.

CONTROL THE DOSAGE OF YOU

One last thought about Dosage, and instead of it being about controlling the intensity of your experiences, it's about controlling the intensity of *you*. I want you to think of new social encounters using the same principle you would with cooking. You don't pour a whole cup of pepper or oregano into a stew; you sprinkle it. It's the same with you and social situations.

There are two aspects to this. One: when we finally get someone to talk to us, we have the tendency to open the floodgates and give the person a megadose of our opinions, enthusiasm, and random thoughts. This can be overwhelming. But if you let the other person do most of the talking, and you're just adding a little flavor, you have a chance to listen, to think, and to be memorable. A dance, a tease, is always more interesting than blasting from a megaphone. Be the seasoning, not the starch.

Two: when we have something we want to say, or a request to make, and the less confident we are, the more we jump right in without any prelude. You may have noticed how poorly this works. For example, if you wanted to borrow money from a friend, you wouldn't just call and say, "Hey, can I borrow three hundred bucks?" You would most likely say hello, and ask how they are, things like that. It's the same with encounters with strangers or coming into new situations. Start small and work your way up to the bigger thing. Gauge when it's time to roll out the big thought or request.

Small Talk

A perfect example of proper Dosage is small talk. Small talk has a negative connotation, which I find bizarre since it is the foundation to social interaction. Few things make people nervous more than a stranger leaping right into a new encounter with "big talk." Imagine walking up to someone new and saying, "How's your marriage going?" or "Have you had any significant deaths in your family recently?" How would you expect that to be received?

Start small, always. It's the polite thing to do, and it shows you're not deranged or so nervous you can't control your mouth. You can open a door with a sledgehammer, but why not use a key instead?

Does small talk seem superficial? Let's hope so. This is where the Dosage step also applies. Always start with a light dose of interest or enthusiasm, not a heavy one. What will happen quite naturally is you will gradually go deeper and deeper and, before you know it, you'll be having an intimate exchange with a complete stranger. But it has to start on the surface.

Don't have a big goal in mind, like you'd like to date that person, go to work for them, become their best friend, hang out with them, or even sit and talk for a while. Let it happen. Trickle it out. Remember, the key is to have no outcome in mind.

Finally, start to notice when other people are good at small talk. Learn from their technique and the words they use. Store those words for your own use later.

Be very careful not to give the person the full Dosage of you in the first encounter. Later we'll talk about creating suspense in a conversation, and this is part of that. Leave them wanting to talk to you more. Doesn't that sound more appealing than running the conversation down to a point where you're both looking around wondering what to say next? Or even worse, where the person is looking for a way to escape because they've overdosed on you in the first serving?

The more relaxed you are, the less likely you are to do this, by the way. And the sooner you will catch yourself doing it and stop. Control the Dosage of you, and they'll be back for more.

CHAPTER 8

EVERY DAY ACTION

The most effective way to reach any goal is to do something every day toward it. It's been proven over and over, and it works because it does these three things:

1. It reprograms your brain with a new self-definition.
2. It moves you toward your goal continuously and steadily builds results.
3. It tricks you into starting and perhaps doing much more than you intended.

REPROGRAMMING YOUR BRAIN

Every Day Action is incredibly powerful because it redefines you to yourself. I'll give you some examples. If you want to be a writer, then write something every day. Your brain will then say, "Oh, it seems I'm a writer now," and it will keep working on your writing in your subconscious throughout the day. Or let's say you want to learn to play piano. If you practice every day, even for five or ten minutes, your brain will say, "I'm a piano player." Same with exercise, learning a language, or eating healthy. Do it only once or twice a week—or when you feel like it—and the brain doesn't make the transition. It defines you as a dabbler, a weekend warrior. In essence, *your actions are what define you to yourself.* Every Day Action cements that definition.

And—big emphasis here—*when you only do it when you feel like it, you'll inevitably do it way, way less!* I'm sure this has been your experience in life already. I guarantee that most of the time you don't feel like working out, but if you're smart, and you want to stay healthy, you do it consistently. I also guarantee you will not feel like doing the Boldness Exercises in this book at first. Every Day Action eliminates that choice.

This is a critical aspect of Every Day Action—you are not deciding to do an exercise that day. You've already decided. It takes no willpower. You don't have to decide whether or not to do it that day. When you dabble, on the other hand, it's a decision battle every time, and the brain is usually looking to conserve energy and reduce stress, so you've got to make a concerted effort to break the inertia that the brain loves so much.

Remember when I talked about creating new neural pathways? Every Day Action is the fastest and most effective way to make that happen.

The actions that you do consistently are what tell your brain and your spirit who you are. Conversely, when you dabble at something, your brain puts that behavior in the low priority category. And your heart is not really in it either.

This same principle has worked for addicts in programs like Alcoholics Anonymous for decades. The scariest thing for an alcoholic is the idea of *never* having a drink again for the rest of their life. It seems impossible. But the idea of not having a drink *today*, that they can deal with. For people kicking an addiction, one day at a time gets them to their goal. It's brilliant and it works.

EVERY DAY ACTION BUILDS RESULTS

One-day-at-a-time action aggregates quickly. For example, thirty days go by and then the Alcoholics Anonymous member gets a one-month chip. It makes them stronger and more determined. Then, day by day, they work their way toward a one-year chip. That reinforces their success and makes it easier to do one more day, even on the hardest days. The days add up to a life of sobriety. My uncle Ed conquered decades of alcoholism this way and had been sober for over forty years when he passed away. One day at a time.

You will experience that same level of reinforcement as you do the Boldness Exercises. The more days you stack up in a row, the more reluctant you'll be to miss a day. You'll eventually find it's much harder to skip a day than to just do a Boldness Exercise. I know this is true for people who exercise consistently too. After a while they can't miss a workout. Their day just doesn't feel right.

This is what will happen to you. You will be bold every day, at least for a few minutes. And it will expand into more and more of your day, and your comfort zone will get bigger and bigger.

Just like with exercise, you don't want to overdo it so much that the next day you feel like you need a break. That's one of the main reasons we have Step 4, controlling the Dosage of the exercises. You want to be able to get back to it every single day, increasing your capacity gradually.

GETTING STARTED

The big bonus is Every Day Action tricks you into starting and doing more than you originally planned. It's one of the best tricks in life.

So often, the hardest thing with challenging tasks is getting started. When you make a nonnegotiable commitment to do something every day, no matter how late it is or how tired you are, you'll find it easier and easier to get started because there's no escaping it, so you might as well get it done.

Starting is the hardest part, and there are some tricks to it.

First, do your exercises early in the day. Doing something first that you are reluctant to do so that it's behind you during the day allows you to enjoy the satisfaction of completion. Often, you discover it wasn't as bad as you were anticipating. You'll be more consistent because you won't find yourself at the end of the day with it still hanging over you, and then maybe putting it off until tomorrow. You certainly have experienced this already in other areas. Doing important tasks early in the day is one of the great tricks to accomplishment in life.

The second step is recording it in your Boldness Journal. Those pages will call to you, wanting to know what you did. It creates an obligation that you need to fulfill.

Third, start easy and work your way up. You may be doing multiple Boldness Exercises in the day, but always start with one you know that you can knock right out, like smiling at a stranger. Then on to bigger and more "discomforting" ones.

Also, if you do it early enough, and it was a success, you'll want to look for a second opportunity. Even if you get a negative response, you'll get energy from it because you did it. Savor that. You've been shot with a Nerf ball. In other words, completely harmless, even though it's aimed right at you. Then, unharmed, you go and do it again. Or get back to it tomorrow with more enthusiasm. Eventually you won't feel satisfied with an exercise until it's a success. As long as you make the attempt every day, the brain continuum will be programmed in.

A few more thoughts about Every Day Action. As a young comedian, Jerry Seinfeld had a simple strategy: he would write jokes every single day, without exception. He knew that inevitably he would accumulate dozens—and finally hundreds—of jokes, and many that didn't work that well. But suddenly there would be an act full of good jokes, and some great ones. And then, a four-decade career.

Similarly, the author Stephen King writes every day for four hours.

Olympic mega-champion Michael Phelps swims six hours a day. Every day, even Sunday, when a lot of other swimmers would take the day off. He figures that the extra day gives him a 14 percent advantage.

In other words, the best in their field know the magic of Every Day Action. Seem like a good idea to imitate the best?

There is another psychological strategy to Every Day Action. Remember my point earlier about how we humans have a limited amount of willpower and can get decision fatigue? When you commit to this step, it stops being a decision whether to do it or not. You KNOW you're going to do it. Every day. Without question. So, you save your willpower for the action itself. It's now reserved energy rather than a daily expenditure, and that's powerful stuff.

One last point about this step. Be sure to let yourself off the hook for missing a day. Just get right back on track. Don't let it drift into two, then three, then five days. Stuff happens in life, I realize. But no matter how crazy your day is, you can find five minutes to do a Boldness Exercise. Don't let busyness become an excuse. Nobody is that busy. I don't know anyone who doesn't waste at least fifteen minutes a day. Use them to become bold instead.

I missed a total of eight days of writing in the four years it took me to complete this book. Two of them were surgeries (I was a little groggy!). But once, when I missed three days in a row, it was actually painful. This is how powerful this step can be in creating a new mindset.

TOOLS FOR EVERY DAY ACTION

Tiny Goals

Planning the steps to boldness incorporates the psychology of Dosage with setting tiny goals. You are programming yourself with something you believe is easily achievable, rather than a huge fantasy goal that you have to convince yourself you will reach. It helps to imagine that big goal, envision it, but most often that recedes while you focus on what you are doing today.

Remember that the PRIDE Method is a matrix. Tiny goals are a merger of the Dosage and Every Day Action steps. An essential part of Dosage control is to make the Every Day Action goal so small, so simple, that you can't *not* do it. The whole design of the Boldness Exercises is to make that daily goal almost impossible to not get to. Some take as little as a minute.

This is part of the trick of Every Day Action. If the goal is so embarrassingly small that we can't use our usual excuses—no time, no energy, no opportunity—then we have to do it.

You will find this technique works with any type of change you want to make in your life. If we trick ourselves into starting by making it seem ridiculous that we're not getting to it, we suddenly find ourselves doing more because it was so easy.

Keep this in mind because if you find yourself with an exercise that does take some time, or that you can't seem to get to for whatever reason, then do a different exercise, a tiny one, so you're doing something every day toward greater boldness. It won't matter that you're not steadily working your way up the scale of intensity. You'll be creating the continuum of activity, and that's what's most important. And your insights will be reinforced.

Your Talisman

As a tool to remind you of your commitment to Every Day Action, I find it helpful to have some sort of body ornament that reminds you to do your exercises. I call it a talisman, which connotes a certain level of magical power, because there is absolutely magic in Every Day Action.

It can be a wristband, a bracelet, a ring, or a necklace. Something you will see that reminds you that you've committed to a path of mastery. It becomes a goal reminder, and you'll be surprised at how effective it is at keeping you consistent.

Remember, this is doing something new, something that is not a habit, and not in your normal behavior. There is nothing more natural as a human being than drifting back to our old behavior and habits. You will have to work to break that pattern by giving yourself cues and rewards. Then it will become a natural habit.

The talisman will help. Putting it on every morning will become a trigger to go out and act boldly that day. Find one that means something special to you, buy it, and wear it. Every day.

Finally, becoming bolder is a goal that affects all your other goals in life. Remember, goals are not dreams. Goals have stairways. That's the big difference. Dreams don't always come true. In fact, more often than not, they don't. That's because a dream without a plan is just a daydream.

Goals create a journey, and along the way you will refine your goals based on the steps you've taken. You'll discover that accomplishing the steps themselves is often the true reward, sometimes even more than the goal itself. Reaching your goal means you need a new one. And then another one. Life becomes more exciting, satisfying, fulfilling.

That statement will be even more true for growing in boldness. Each day that you feel a little bolder, a little less inhibited, you will be—OK, let me put the biggest goal right out there—happier. Not some "put on a happy face" happier, but "deep down I like myself and how I move through the world" happier.

Billionaire Bill Gates has said we often overestimate what can be accomplished in a year and underestimate what can be accomplished in a decade. I'll adapt that by saying we underestimate how fast we can change if we just work at something every single day.

THE PRIDE METHOD: FINAL THOUGHTS

That's it—we've covered each stage of the PRIDE Method in depth, so you can see how they interact with each other to help you overcome your under-confidence and barrier beliefs. In Part III, as promised, we'll delve into practical tools, concepts, and mental exercises that will help you prepare for the Boldness Exercises and becoming bolder in general.

Here's my last takeaway for the PRIDE Method: get yourself a wing person. I don't mean this in its normal context of someone who helps you pick up someone in a club or a bar. I see this person more as someone who holds you accountable rather than someone who makes it easier for you socially. When you are doing the Boldness Exercises, an ally can be a huge help.

The important thing for the wing person to know is the difference between a push and a nudge. It should be someone more like a friend who encourages you to go for something. It is the difference between soft pressure on your back and a full-force shove. It's not someone who's going to "show you how it's done." That's worthless, in my mind, because you are not them. You need to figure out how *you* will do it.

So, recruit a wing person. Explain the PRIDE Method to them. Let them know what you're trying to achieve with the Boldness Exercises. That way you've declared it publicly and can't waver from the commitment. Just don't lean on them. As I said, the purpose of your wing person is simple: to hold you accountable. Their task is making sure you do your exercises every day.

They do not have to be with you whenever you do the exercises. I want you flying solo most of the time. But they should know what you're intending to do, and they're going to check in with you. Occasionally you might need a little wind beneath your wings, someone to prop you up, nudge you forward, or check your teeth for salad remains, so bring them along sometimes.

Especially as you first begin the exercises, if it gets you out of the house, by all means use a wing person. But they need to understand that you're trying to take some baby steps, and it may be embarrassing for you to admit how maladjusted you feel.

They are your training wheels, but they are not your safe harbor. Your goal is to fail, which reverses your expectation. It is critical not to hide from the crowd with your wing person. This is what you've always done, and you're trying to get beyond it. I will tell you that I know exactly what that feeling is, like you're adrift, alone in an ocean of strangers, your stomach clenched, clammy all over, and tongue-tied. I will also tell you that for most situations, that is a distant memory for me.

Also, asking someone to be your wing person is a bold move in and of itself. So, recruit a wing person, but with these guidelines:

- Their job is to nudge, not to shove.
- They don't show you how it's done.
- They let you fail.
- They never shame you or are disappointed in you.

Also, they remind you of the PRIDE Method steps. They prepare you, relax you, and give you the Insight that you're not going to die. They make sure the Dosage of the experience is proper, and they remind you to be consistent and do the exercises daily.

Here is my promise if you practice the PRIDE Method and do the Boldness Exercises diligently: you will reach a point where you trust in the unexpected. This is the dream plateau in your boldness. Once you come to trust that putting yourself out there yields delightful and unexpected experiences, your life will be more enriched and satisfying than you thought possible.

The difference between you and bold people is you encounter situations and ask what might go wrong. Bold people never ask that question, especially about a simple human encounter. They trust that it will go right, and they also don't care when it doesn't. That's a powerful place to be. And more in touch with the truth, which is that it doesn't matter, and nothing really can go so wrong that you would die of shame and humiliation.

Finally, let me give you a couple of classic boldness examples that show the fun that can occur.

My ex-wife, Mira, has developed her boldness to a high degree. One time we were walking the streets of Portland around 11:00 p.m., and through a window she saw this bakery with people working and fresh donuts laid out. She was trying to figure out how to get one of those donuts, even though they were closed. They saw her eager face and gestures, and eventually let us in and gave her one. They explained that they were a Japanese pop-up kitchen using the space to do a *Twin Peaks*-themed dinner the next night, Valentine's Day. She then managed to get two seats at that dinner, even though they were booked up. It turned out to be a wonderful and totally unique, unanticipated experience, simply because she put herself out there.

A few years ago, I was attending a revival of the sixties musical *Hair* on Broadway with some friends. During the intermission, I overheard that during the encore the cast would invite some of the audience up onstage to sing and dance with them.

So, as the play ended, I made my way to the side of the stage, racing down from my balcony seat. Sure enough, they invited a group of us up, and I got to dance on a Broadway stage surrounded by hippie cast members, looking out at the audience all on their feet clapping and singing along. Everyone I was sitting with was wondering where I went until someone spotted me onstage. It was beautiful. Singular. And I'd have been so mad at myself if I had let that moment pass and stayed in my seat.

This is what can happen when you are bold. Delightful, unexpected experiences will pop up, like a Japanese kitchen on the streets of Portland or a moment on a Broadway stage. These are simple and insignificant examples, but you add a few dozen of these up, and suddenly life gets pretty darn interesting.

PART III

FOUNDATIONS

CHAPTER 9

GUIDING PRINCIPLES

The following are ten guiding principles in your path to boldness. They are also interspersed throughout the book in other forms, but I want to spell them out in clear, simple terms here. These principles will spark you, motivate you, and guide you in your choices. In my experience, they are valuable beyond becoming bolder. As standalone thoughts, they are keys to living a full and fulfilling life.

GUIDING PRINCIPLE #1:
THE PRIME DIRECTIVE—BE THE VOICE OF UPLIFTMENT

If you're a *Star Trek* fan, you recall the prime directive, the rule for all of Star Fleet prohibiting them from interfering with the development of alien civilizations. I have a different prime directive for you, one that is perhaps the most powerful guiding principle I've ever discovered. It's this:

Lift people up.

In other words, in every encounter, make the other person feel better about themselves. I call it *being the voice of upliftment.*

Now I know some of you are saying, "Wait a minute. Bold people make me uncomfortable. They don't make me feel better about myself." I need to point out that they are making you uncomfortable when you are watching them, not when they are interacting with you. Big difference.

First of all, they're not *trying* to make you feel uncomfortable. That's what's important. They are trying to create a good time, or they are chasing their dreams with unrelenting passion. In doing so, they are setting an example for you. The discomfort they are causing you is a gift they are giving you, if you just decide to receive it.

If you pay closer attention, when you interact with a bold person directly, they do tend to make you feel better about yourself. They are liberal with their compliments, curious about you, and generally positive. This is the true essence of their charisma.

They are pursuing their fulfilling life with all their energy, enthusiasm, and daring. They're confident. And *they are no different than you.* That truth is the real gift. You may not feel better about yourself when you merely observe them, but you will look back someday and thank them for their example, if you choose to learn from it, if you use it as inspiration and motivation. Then you will feel genuinely, permanently better about yourself.

That's what you'll be doing someday when you are bold. You'll be making some people uncomfortable and embarrassed for you. How silly they will seem to you then. But mostly, you'll be the voice of upliftment.

The prime directive is powerful because of the effect it has on people—you're making them feel better about themselves. Don't worry about making yourself feel good. You will start to feel amazing things if you make other people feel good about themselves, and amazing, positive people will gravitate toward you.

The prime directive isn't only about making people feel good about themselves. It's also about breaking out of *your* prison of negativity. Think back to Chapter 3, where we talked about crutches. We discussed how negativity becomes a crutch on which we lean to feel better about ourselves. That negativity leaks into our thoughts, our opinions, our speech patterns. Many people complain, criticize, and accentuate the negative all the time, often to complete strangers.

The prime directive asks you to change that. One of the greatest challenges in life is to eliminate the negative from your speech. It is also one of the most transformational. Day by day, sentence by sentence, express yourself positively. Become the voice of upliftment.

Remember when I talked about new neural pathways being formed when you change your behavior? This applies completely to this principle. If you find yourself going negative, stop. Listen to yourself and train yourself to come up with alternatives. Don't start sentences with things like, "I hate…" or "I can't believe how bad…"

This will be an interesting process of consciously registering your thoughts and what you express. You may be surprised at how often and how easily you go negative. If you find it almost impossible to stop at certain times, then perhaps your style will be to put a positive spin on a negative comment, like, "This rain may be miserable, yet it beats having a drought."

This will be a whole lot harder than you think, but you MUST do it. Once you do, you will hear how often other people use the negative as their primary medium of exchange. This is code that needs to be overwritten or erased so that the new lines of positive code can spiral your life upward.

So consciously, continually offer positive stuff. I don't mean things like, "Thank God it's Friday." Slackers don't impress many people and letting them know that you hate work, or reminding them that they do, doesn't improve society. It's easy to come up with the negative, but when you offer something positive, people will rethink their tendency to go negative.

Be the voice of upliftment. It will radiate far and wide, trust me.

GUIDING PRINCIPLE #2:
IF YOU WANT DIFFERENT RESULTS,
DO SOMETHING DIFFERENT

The key word here is *do*. Action must be taken. Wishing doesn't work.

I'm going to spell out what may seem obvious, but it's what most people ignore all the time in their personal behavior, and that's this: if something isn't working for you, *try something different!* Don't keep doing the same things hoping for a different result. That's not only unscientific, it's crazy. Many people live their lives wishing, hoping, and *expecting* the world to change its response to them. They think things should somehow magically be different without them changing any of their behavior. Once again, that's crazy.

Becoming bold, acting with high self-confidence and self-esteem, means doing things differently than you've ever done them so you can get radically different results. Just reading this book will do very little. Doing the Boldness Exercises will change everything.

Remember, you are not just learning but also unlearning. You are writing over the stale code, the programming that got you this far but is now holding you back. Don't waste time with regret; just move on. That code likely protected you, as you were not old enough or mature enough to deal with what came at you. Doesn't matter. You will unlearn those messages and learn to become bold.

GUIDING PRINCIPLE #3:
BE PROUD

You've tried shame; now try pride. Not some preening vanity, but feeling good about yourself as you move through the world. Aim to be that person you want to be proud of. There's nothing wrong with that. Let that negative connotation go. Why wouldn't you want to live a life you're proud of?

GUIDING PRINCIPLE #4:
EMBRACE FAILURE

Expect to stumble before you walk and trip when you run. This is how you learn and grow. When you succeed, it will be a delicious surprise instead of the expectation that you used to need to motivate you. Failing only makes *you* a failure if you decide to give up. A boxer in training will get punched in the face if he drops his guard. Does this make him quit boxing? No. His failure to protect his face is painfully indicated by a smack in the head. So he learns to keep his guard up. *He* is not a failure. He's a learner. Stacking up failure is how we learn almost everything.

No one bats 1.000. That's a baseball term that is relevant to all of life. Baseball legend Babe Ruth hit 714 home runs in his career. He also struck out 1,330 times. He was quite certain he was more likely to strike out than hit a homer. Did it keep him from swinging the bat at a withering fast-ball? No. He famously said, "Every strikeout gets me closer to a home run."

Telemarketers know they will need to make one hundred cold calls to get five people on the phone and sell to one of them.

Professional poker players know if you never get bluffed out, then you're not calling enough hands. You're playing too cautiously, and you won't ever win big.

Gymnasts fail to stick landings hundreds of times, maybe thousands, on their way to the Olympics.

Whatever analogy works for you, apply it, because it's the guideline to all success. You try, you fail, you learn, you get better. In this case, it's about your whole life, not just a game. The goal in almost everything in life is to make mistakes, to fail, to strike out. That way you know you're taking enough chances.

I heard a podcast interview with Matt Mullenweg, the developer of the highly successful software WordPress, where he said that the history of the human race can be summed up in one word: mistakes. That's the essential concept here. The goal is to endure the discomfort of making mistakes, and translate it—transform it, even—into learning. That is the true essence of confidence. Underlying genuine confidence is the courage to be uncomfortable, the willingness to take risks, which by definition means you might fail.

Embracing failure is the key to the Boldness Exercises. Most of the time, by design, you are expecting nothing in return from these social encounters. Not even a smile or even a response. Because then everything positive you receive is a bonus. Failure is part of the plan. When it's part of the plan, pretty soon it's part of the fun!

GUIDING PRINCIPLE #5:
NEUTRALIZE REJECTION

This is an extension of the fourth principle, because many times the failures will come in the form of some type of rejection. It's important enough to be its own principle. I want you to develop what I call your *rejection callus*. This requires a combination of the critical insight that most rejection is not about you and the repeated exposure to rejection so that it becomes harmless.

GUIDING PRINCIPLE #6:
SUSPEND YOUR JUDGMENT OF OTHER PEOPLE

Stop creating truths about people out of thin air, or casual observation, or bias. You're wrong so often it's a waste of energy, and you will miss out on experiences and people who will bring unexpected reward to your life.

For most of my life, I had judgments about people when I first met them. What was worse is I had judgments about people before I even met them, just by looking at them, and I formulated opinions based on what they wore, how they looked, or their demeanor.

Sound familiar? I'm not sure why most of us do this but, if I had to choose, I would say insecurity is the primary driver. We're a bunch of profilers. The trouble was, when I took the time to get to know the person, I found I was wrong about 85 percent of the time. I'm hoping you've discovered the same thing.

It's time to let that behavior go. Stop judging people with so little information. Their height, their weight, their attire, or their facial expression is not the whole story. Not even a tiny part. Not to mention that most of the time you just have a snapshot of them, not their whole life. This could be the worst day of their life, or the best. Or anywhere in between. How would you know? It's not helping you to do this. Suspending judgment is the first step in a new encounter. Be open to who they might be. Judgment will block your positivity. I can attest to that.

Also, people don't reveal themselves completely in the first moments. Start with a blank slate, and you'll be surprised at how often you'll find the person interesting. I'm not saying you're going to like everyone. That's not possible or even necessary. But just as you can't judge someone's criminal proclivities by their skin color, you can't know everything about someone, or categorize them accurately, in the first thirty seconds.

Suspending judgment also gives you the chance to discover people that you wouldn't normally associate with. I once chatted with a bald man wearing a dress and lipstick who happened to be sitting next to me in a bar. No big deal. Casual conversation. After twenty minutes, he had become a real person to me, not a stereotype. I came away from the exchange feeling uplifted because he was funny and certainly lived life differently than most people I knew. I hadn't let my judgment prevent me from meeting someone, and that felt pretty good.

A critical part of Preparation is to suspend your judgment of new people, and let your curiosity take over instead. Be in discovery mode rather than assumption mode. You'll be surprised at how much more fun that is.

GUIDING PRINCIPLE #7:
LET GO OF OTHER PEOPLE'S OPINIONS
AND JUDGMENTS ABOUT YOU

The bolder you become, the more people will have sneering judgments about you. Most often these are rooted in their insecurity, resentment, and jealousy. They secretly would like to be you. But this is the Insight: people constantly have judgments about other people's actions and behavior *as if their lives are perfect and they've figured everything out.* Guess what? They haven't. No one has. So, ignore them.

The greatest achievers in the world had people who detested them, railed against their every action, and belittled their every achievement. Franklin Delano Roosevelt, who guided the US out of the Great Depression and then led us successfully through World War II, had major detractors, so much so that, after he died, they amended the Constitution so that a president could serve only two terms. (He was elected four times.) Did those harsh judgments stop him from forging the New Deal or launching D-Day? No. He gathered the opinions that mattered to him and ignored the rest.

I'll give you a more common example of strangers' opinions. If you are in your car, driving slowly because you are lost, does it really matter that the person behind you thinks you're an idiot? Does that actually *make* you an idiot, or are you simply in an unfamiliar situation? Guess what? We all are sometimes. Do you really care what other drivers think about your driving? I doubt it. So why let *any* of their other erroneous and uninformed opinions bother you?

When I do a speaking engagement, I know that someone in the audience is certain to think I'm way off base, another will think I'm a hustler or crackpot, and another won't be able to think beyond the tie choice I've made. Someone may even fall asleep. I care about my audience because I want to help as many people as possible, but I know I'm not going to get everyone to love me. If just one person comes up at the end of my talk and says, "Thank you. That was just what I needed to hear right now," I'm good. It doesn't matter that some people didn't appreciate what I had to say.

You will achieve boldness only when you stop caring about unimportant opinions. And *only you get to decide who is important.* Fairly empowering, isn't it?

GUIDING PRINCIPLE #8:
MOST OF THE TIME, NOTHING BAD HAPPENS

This is the reality when it comes to being bold. All those terrible things that you imagine might happen never happen. Worse, we decide to call something bad when it isn't. Embarrassment can be funny. Rejection can elicit empathy for us. Actual bad things can happen in your life, but not because you are bold. Usually, because you weren't.

GUIDING PRINCIPLE #9:
YOUR BRAIN NEEDS REGULAR WASHING

You need to overwrite the negative messages you tell yourself with positive ones. Change every "I can't" to "I can." Every "I'm not" to "I am." Just say the opposite. You might call it brainwashing yourself, but most of our brains need a good washing.

Rinse out that bad programming the second you hear yourself replaying it. Brainwashing is actually rather fun to do. You simply take something you've said you hate or that you're not good at, and tell yourself, out loud, every day, that you love it or you are really good at it.

Some examples of these reversals:

"I'm great at math."
"I love to dance."
"I look forward to public speaking."

"I remember people's names easily."

"I'm always calm when I meet new people."

"I'm naturally friendly."

"I assume the best of everyone."

You will find that in about two weeks, if you do it four or five times a day, you will have reprogrammed yourself. Dig up some of your bad lines of code and overwrite them one at a time.

GUIDING PRINCIPLE #10:
NEVER BE RUDE, INCONSIDERATE, OR CRUEL

I do not advocate getting ahead at other people's expense. That's not what true boldness and self-confidence are about. You will undoubtedly make people uncomfortable, but that is not the same as being rude or inconsiderate. True boldness is founded in a belief in abundance, which means you don't have to harm anyone else to achieve your goals or your dreams.

When you get there, it doesn't mean you get to look down on everyone. Cruel behavior is the sign of a lost soul, in my mind.

When I talk about being bold, I'm not suggesting a lack of manners, or discourtesy, or rudeness. I'm hoping you have enough sense of propriety and decorum to behave appropriately in all social situations. But, many times, we use being considerate as an excuse for being reticent, not taking action, or not making a bold move. You tell yourself you don't want to make people uncomfortable, which is just your excuse for not being bold. Most bold moves don't harm anyone, unless it's their ego or the fact that they are envious of the bold person.

You are not five years old. You're not supposed to sit still and be silent, like a child who has been told not to speak unless spoken to. That's just misguided rules for an obsolete society. So some of my Boldness Exercises may seem a bit crazy, and may indeed make some people you encounter uncomfortable, but in reality the only person "harmed" would be you, because you put yourself out there and maybe got arrested or at least felt a bit embarrassed. (Please don't get arrested!)

I've found that many people get uncomfortable because they need everyone to follow their rules. I personally don't give a tiny damn about what those people think. They're trapped in their judgment of others, and that is their problem, not yours or mine. You will make some people uncomfortable. Guess what? It's not a crime. In fact, it speaks more to their issues than it does to your behavior.

And guess what? If you're shy, some people out there already think you're rude. Your hesitance to be social very often is misread as impolite, or worse. You not saying hello, or asking or learning people's names, can easily be interpreted as being aloof or snooty. Not everyone gives you the benefit of the doubt, especially if you don't seem distressed and are holding your anxiety inside.

If you don't cross the line a few times, then you're not trying hard enough. Please don't be rude or hurtful or do anything harmful to anyone. But pushing your boldness boundaries is going to get a reaction from people, especially those who know you and have a different expectation of you. That's the point. You're making yourself uncomfortable and maybe some of them too. They'll live. And you'll live more fully.

CHAPTER 10

SOCIAL SKILLS AND POWER TOOLS

I n Chapter 5, we talked about the first stage of Preparation, which included behavior guidelines, tips, and techniques to ground you in social situations. This chapter will tackle these in depth. Think of them as arrows in your social quiver.

Remember, the true purpose of the PRIDE step of Preparation, along with the Boldness Exercises, is to make things reflexive. All of these tips will come in handy in the exercises and will eventually become so natural for you that you won't need to think about them. You'll already be prepared.

SOCIAL SKILLS

Here are some social skills that many people are not taught to do by their parents, teachers, or friends. If you already understand and do these consistently, great. You're ahead of about half the population. If not, then here they are so you can practice.

Basics

To start with, I'm going to tell you a little secret. You will never starve if you master the first two things: smiling and eye contact. You will always be able to find a job in the retail or hospitality industries, as these are the baseline skills for those jobs, and also how people most succeed in them. It also is one of the key reasons people get hired for *any* job. I'm not saying that these two skills alone will make you rich. But rich is relative, employed is not. That's why they are first on the list of basics.

1. **Smile.** It's friendly. It's disarming. It's inviting. Just as not smiling isn't any of those things. You undoubtedly have some story playing in your head that tells you that to smile when you don't feel happy is phony. Is that why everyone is smiling at people? They're happy all the time? No. You've just given yourself a lovely cop-out so you don't have to develop social skills because you're being "real." Nonsense. Smiling is no different than shaking hands. Do you shake hands with someone because of a need for physical contact? No. You do it to be courteous and respectful. Smile to be friendly, to shoot some light at someone, even a stranger. It costs nothing.

2. **Make eye contact.** When you first meet people, look them in the eye. You don't have to hold it indefinitely, as that can be creepy anyway, but not looking them in the eye when first meeting shows your utter lack of confidence. Doing it connects.

3. **Shake hands firmly.** That means you don't hand them a limp set of fingers. Shy people often have a cautious and often wet handshake. If you do, dry your hand first, and then give a good single squeeze. I'm amazed at how many people's parents never taught them how to shake hands. This is the same for men and women. A dainty handshake as a woman creates a distinct impression that you are delicate and need to be treated that way.

Maybe that's your goal, but I would abandon that for a path to boldness instead. Boldness creates independence rather than dependence. Also, as a woman, don't overcompensate by shaking hands like you're a longshoreman. For both men and women, it's not a grip contest, it's a greeting. And don't linger. A double pump at the most, and then let go.

4. **Say hi.** I even prefer it to hello, because hi leaves your mouth in an upturned smile. Make a habit of saying it to anyone who makes eye contact with you and anyone you want to meet. Don't wait for them to say it first. (Where is the boldness in that?) If they don't say it back, keep smiling and move on. Don't ascribe any meaning to it—you don't know what their response really means, so forget it. Don't decide to crawl back into your shell.

5. **Speak up.** Many people, especially shy people, have a tendency not to speak audibly when they first meet someone. Volume is confidence. Low volume gives the opposite message.

6. **Know when to walk away.** Watch for clues in facial expressions and body language when in a conversation. Don't confuse politeness with genuine interest. Some people are either not interested or lose interest. Don't take it personally, just politely excuse yourself. Don't wait until their eyes glaze over, or for the uncomfortable silence that often occurs. Also, don't say, "Well, I guess that's a lull, so maybe we should mingle," or some dumbass comment like that. Be definitive. "Would you excuse me? I just saw someone I want to catch while they're available," or "Would you mind if I dashed over and chatted with that person? It was really great to meet you." It lets people know that you don't need to fill your entire tank at their pump. And you haven't turned it into an awkward, "Well, I guess there's nothing more to talk about," moment. They will be a bit surprised that you were

the one who broke off the exchange and be more impressed with your perceptiveness. All of life is an awareness test. Pay attention, and you will always be learning and improving.

The LASER Technique

One of the things I urge you to develop—it's a bit like a superpower—is the ability to make someone feel *special*. This is actually an elevation to the prime directive (i.e., Guiding Principle #1). You will use it as you choose, not necessarily toward everyone, but you'll be surprised how effective it is, and you'll likely use it more often than you think. It is an amazing life skill. Anyone who people consider charismatic has mastered it.

Some people have refined this elevation to an extremely high degree. For example, years ago, I met former president Bill Clinton at a fundraiser, when he was running for president the first time. I marveled at his uncanny ability to focus completely on the person he was meeting. I watched him do it that evening over and over with almost two hundred people, one at a time. It was remarkable. When it was my turn, I felt like I was the only person in the room. I believe it was one of the major reasons he was elected.

This is a superpower life skill: to make someone feel like they are the only person in the room. How? The steps are simple.

1. **Look at the person.** And only them. At no point do you look away, especially beyond or around them to someone else. People can tell instantly when your eyes are focused on something besides them. You may notice that they sometimes turn to see what you are looking at instead of them.
2. **Actively listen.** Focus completely on being interested in what they are saying, and only that. If you are thinking about what you want to say next, they can tell.
3. **Stay focused on them.** Don't let your attention wander. Stay completely focused on them to the end of the interaction.

4. **End well.** When you do finally decide to break away, don't look away first and then say some equivalent of, "Well, I've got to be going now." Look straight at them and say something like, "It was great to meet you. I'm going to remember what you said about global warming, Stan. I've got a few other people to meet." Shake hands, squeeze their shoulder, or hug them if you're a hugger. Then look away as you move away, not before.

5. **Remember them.** The next time you see them, remember their name and some detail about them. You'll blow their mind.

Think of it by the acronym LASER:

Look at them.
Actively listen.
Stay focused.
End well.
Remember them.

To give you more detail, let's break that final communication down:

"It was great to meet you." That communicated that you were at the wrap-up.

"... global warming." You showed them you were listening.

"Stan." You remembered their name.

"I've got a few other people to meet." That's your gracious exit line.

If you can maintain total focus on the person, you will be astounded at how people will respond. You will not have to do it for long. It works within minutes.

The LASER Technique is a master move in superboldness. Learn it.

Let Go of the Agenda

Having an agenda to your interaction, that is, an ulterior motive, diminishes the connection you are trying to create. This is not as obviously practical as the other tips in this section, but it has a big impact on how you are received in social situations and the success of your endeavors.

Do you remember Emily from Chapter 3? The sweet, little girl who turned and started chatting to me at a restaurant? Who spelled out her name: E-M-I-L-Y? She struck up a conversation easily, and I found it charming. But therein lies a key lesson. There was no hidden agenda for Emily. She was purely being social. And I couldn't resist it. I'll say it again: *There was no hidden agenda for Emily.*

Emily offers a very powerful message here. Most people, when they are approached by someone whose intentions are innocent, are friendly and responsive in return. Conversely, when it is perceived as something other than an innocent social exchange, when an ulterior or hidden motive is suspected, then the dynamic changes completely.

Which means that if you come off as needy, desperate, aggressive, aloof, conniving, or any number of other attitudinal malfunctions, you will get a negative reaction. It is not the other person's fault. It's yours.

It's the same thing that happens when you are trying to impress people or when you are *trying* to be interesting. You know when you're trying to be interesting, don't you? You memorized a joke. Or told a rehearsed story about yourself. Or you went on a tangent about the news of the day, without registering the appeal of the information. You are not trying to inform; you are trying to impress. That's not good. That's the wrong motive. Your goal is to *connect*, and trying to impress people short-circuits that. Anytime you catch yourself trying to impress people, slam on the brakes.

In time, as you practice the Boldness Exercises and move up on the boldness scale, you *will* become interesting. That will happen as you develop the skill, not just because you *decide* to be interesting. So approach new social encounters without an agenda, with the same ease and charm as Emily. Remember, you're expecting rejection, you've redefined "failure" as "learning," and all you're looking to do is connect.

If you find you can't do any or all of these social skills, the PRIDE Method will help you with each of them, so don't be frustrated and say, "If I could do those things, I wouldn't be reading this book!" You'll get there. I'll get you there. Faster than you expect.

POWER TOOLS

Beyond the social skills, part of your Preparation is to develop skills that will transform your interactions. I call these Power Tools. They range from fairly obvious to more subtle, but each work to create impactful, memorable interactions and open doors that previously would have been locked to you. They will amplify and accelerate you as you do your Boldness Exercises, but they are also life skills, useful every day. They are:

1. Learning Names
2. Asking Questions
3. Upgrading Your Default Expression
4. Key Words and Compliments
5. Adding to Yes
6. Saying the Unexpected
7. Creating Suspense

Power Tool #1: Learning Names

We all love to hear our names. It's music to our ears.

Naturally, if you tell yourself you're bad at remembering people's names, you will be. The fact is, most of the time we can remember names if we associate them with something about the person and repeat their name a few times in the first interaction. It also requires active listening, which we neglect very often when we first meet someone and hear their name for the first time. So…

Step 1: Tell yourself you are good at remembering names. Rewrite that bad line of code.

Step 2: When someone tells you their name, repeat it back immediately.

Step 3: Find something unique about them to associate with their name, maybe even make a rhyme or some other mnemonic (memory trigger) to go with it, like, "Jim goes to the gym a lot."

Step 4: Get the pronunciation right or ask exactly how to say their name. Ask them to spell it, even, especially if you are more literal than auditory in your learning.

Step 5: Use their name as often as possible in the first encounter.

Step 6: Tell them your name.

Step 7: If you forget their name, ask them again.

This last step can be done politely and cleverly. Say something like, "I was so distracted by how well-dressed you are that I forgot your name." See the trick? You embedded a compliment into your request for them to repeat their name. Now you are saying that they are interesting rather than forgettable.

Don't say, "I'm terrible at remembering names. What's yours again?" because this violates Step 1. You could say instead, "I'm usually good at remembering names, but yours was so easy that I managed to forget it."

Relaxing is a critical part of remembering people's names. The more nervous you are, the worse your memory and even your hearing will be. Breathe. Listen. Repeat their name. You can also aid your memory by saying, "My favorite niece's name is Stephanie," or some other association with someone you know with that name. Or, if it's true, say, "I've never heard that name before. It's really beautiful/unique/interesting!"

If this is still a challenge for you, search for Jim Kwik's YouTube video, or even better, take one of his weekend courses. You will get significantly better at learning names very quickly. Hence, his last name.

Power Tool #2: Asking Questions

Your simplest solution to making a connection in any new conversation is to ask the person questions. Questions are magic. They are powerful. The subtext is "I'm interested in what you think" or "I'm interested in who you are." And it leads to an exchange. You get to listen and learn, and then add to it.

To be interest*ing*, be interest*ed*. This aphorism has been around for decades, and it applies as much now as it ever did. You don't have to come up with a load of interesting stories, jokes, and comments to have people appreciate you and find you interesting.

I can't tell you how many situations I've been in where all I did was essentially ask a question, listen to the answer, and then ask another question, for the entire conversation. Later I would hear that the person thought I was really interesting, even though I had hardly said anything to the person.

Allow yourself the release of being interested in someone else, and they will respond. Listen actively, and learn who they are, what they care about, and what's happened to them that was meaningful.

There are two pitfalls in asking questions:

1. Asking yes or no questions. These don't lead anywhere. You're forced to ask another question or hope that they start to elaborate on their one-word answer. Go deeper.
2. Asking questions that aren't really questions. The most obvious of these is "How you doin'?" These too are questions that elicit a one-word answer or a nontruth like, "I'm fine" or "I'm doing great."

Asking good questions is an art. But it starts simply. Here are some good examples:

- "Did anything interesting happen to you this week?"

- "What do you think about…?"…an event of the day, or some other topic. And here, you don't reveal your bias. Leave it open-ended.
- "Where did you find that unique shirt/tie/coat/skirt/dress/handbag?" Or whatever. Something that might spark a story. They are usually wearing something unique for a reason.

Get the idea? Develop this skill and be attuned to the responses so that your next question goes deeper or allows them to reveal more about themselves, what they care about, what's important to them, and what experiences they've had.

There are certain situations where you would ask someone what they do for a living, but this isn't a go-to question all the time. I almost never lead with it, unless I'm at a specific networking event where it is pretty much what everyone is asking. That question has the possibility of sounding like you are trying to assess their worthiness. Some of the most interesting people I've met were between jobs or their job was the least interesting thing about them.

Asking good questions is an art form but, like all art forms, starting simple is the way to go, just as sometimes the simplest melody or drawing is the most universal in its appeal. This is a powerful life skill—develop it and doors will open.

Along with asking questions, you will need to start actively listening. That means listening closely enough where you could repeat what the person said almost word for word. The key to this is not thinking about what you're going to say next or anything else.

Just listen. It's hard to do. But when you listen with the intention of gathering information about the person, it keeps you from interrupting them. Few people enjoy being interrupted. It makes you seem overeager and even rude. Listening closely also gives you the freedom to look at their posture and facial expressions as they speak. If all you can think about is your next response, then you're not doing any of those things, and you will not pick up important cues about what the person cares about and how they are responding to you.

Active listening is crucial to do when you first meet someone, and as a general life skill it is in the top three.

Power Tool #3: Upgrading Your Default Expression

Every one of us has a default expression, which is what our face looks like most of the time.

How often do you smile? How many times a day?

"Oh, no," you're probably thinking. "He's not really going to give me the whole 'put on a happy face' pitch again, is he?"

I am, but not just for the usual reasons. The real reason is because it's been proven that smiling more makes you happier. Not smiling because you feel like smiling, but consciously *choosing* to smile even when you don't feel like it. It actually changes the endorphin levels in your system. Putting on a smile makes you *feel* happier. Also, I'm challenging you to do something different if what you're currently doing isn't working.

So, check your face. This goes beyond smiling. It's what you look like when you're not smiling. What is your default expression? By that I mean, when you are just sitting there, relaxed, not communicating with anyone. Is it neutral? Is it inviting, happy, warm, friendly, or is it sad, frowning, grouchy, judgmental? Do you find yourself scowling a good part of the time? Or just sitting there with a downturned mouth? If so, I want you to try to catch yourself at it and deliberately bring some lightness, some positivity, into your face.

Notice what you look like in pictures when you're not posing so that you can see what your default expression is. You could even ask someone. I was kind of shocked when people told me years ago that I looked angry, even though I wasn't feeling that way. Not good. So I changed it.

Now, whenever I notice someone with a grim, sad, or grouchy expression, I use it as a cue to actively reset my own. It's easy to droop into that kind of face, and it's not what you want to show the world. We all have that face we make when we are checking our smartphones. Downturned mouth, double chin, head tilted down. Or worse, mouth hanging open. Lovely.

Gravity is at work here too. You'll have to use some facial muscles to lift up and retrain your face to look happier.

Right now, look in the mirror. Relax your face completely. Let your jaw loosen and your lips separate. Now be honest about your features. Does your mouth turn down naturally? If it does, then you have to make an effort to smile more and lift it. Or you may think you're smiling when in fact your smile is a straight horizontal line. Or maybe your default face looks stern. I have a friend, a great big guy with a square jaw that almost makes him look like Frankenstein's monster. He honestly looks mean and a little frightening. Until he smiles. Then he beams. His whole face changes and you are drawn into his fantastic open smile.

Reset your expression. Reset your face. It is what you project to the world. Just think about how you respond to other people's expressions. Listen to your internal monologue, your judgments about them. They are almost always at least partially based on their facial expressions. That's exactly what's happening to you too.

So let's change that. Smile more. A lot more. Upgrade your default face. And use other people's unpleasant expressions to trigger you to reset yours to something happier, more appealing, starting today.

Power Tool #4: Using Key Words and Compliments

Some words are much less appropriate than others in an initial encounter. They carry too much juice, too much intensity, or they are hard to interpret, or easy to misinterpret.

Look at this list of adjectives and see how you would rate them if someone you just met used them to describe you. As in, "You seem like a _____ person." Fill in that blank and see how each one feels. See how these various words strike you.

Happy

Genuine

Calm

Intense

Friendly

Harmless

Inviting

Attractive

Stylish

Athletic

Comfortable

Cool

Hip

Exotic

Sensuous

Marvelous

Skinny

Sexy

Experienced

Kind

How did some of them hit you? Did "sensuous" strike you as a bit odd? Some of the ones that are about appearance can be very tricky and risky. How about "harmless"? Do you think you could make that work? And "experienced"? Might that be taken the wrong way?

The reason for this exercise is that complimenting early on in an encounter is a powerful tool. But it has to feel genuine, not excessively flattering, and not weird or creepy. Do you sense where the line is? And of course, what happens when we skip PRIDE Step 2, Relaxing, is our brain will feed us the wrong word. Find some words that you feel comfortable with, that you can say believably, and that don't push the boundaries of a healthy exchange.

Remember that the unexpected is memorable. Here are some that I consider unique and also less focused on appearance:

Observant

Perceptive

Intriguing

Intuitive

Energetic

Relaxed

Dynamic

Serene

Playful

Fun-loving

Worldly

Wise

Adverb Power

There is also something wonderful about a well-chosen adverb. Imagine these preceding one of the adjectives above:

Uniquely

Surprisingly

Intriguingly (aloof/observant/reserved/fashionable)

Distractingly (pretty/attractive/well-dressed/confident/intelligent)

Especially

Genuinely

Adverbs can elevate a simple adjective and at the same time diminish the intensity. For example, telling someone they are "uniquely attractive" somehow seems less like you're hitting on them and more like you're giving them a compliment.

Remember, when you say something like this, there is seldom any momentum in the dialogue. The person may thank you and turn away. Or not even acknowledge you. Or they might appreciate it to a surprising degree. Or it may lead to a lengthier interaction. The point is, you won't know ahead of time, and nothing can teach you how to predict how every single person will react. Therefore, you can't concern yourself with it, just learn from it.

If used during a Boldness Exercise, you will be moving on, no matter what. It will be practice, not a full encounter. But if it's in a conversation, using a compliment is often better a few more sentences into the encounter than right off the bat.

I am excessively biased against clichés (like "right off the bat"), and this has not necessarily been a good thing for me. There are many times when clichés are perfectly appropriate and actually make people feel comfortable. I like to say something unique, but not every situation requires that. It can put someone in a position where they feel like they have to be as clever. Remember the goal, which is to open up the conversation.

Try to develop a repertoire of words that are unique, positive, complimentary, but not bizarre or esoteric. When you find out what best rolls off your tongue, these words are reusable, so build up your working vocabulary. If you have clichés that you can make work, add them as well.

Most of all, focus on compliments. Compliments are conversation gold.

Compliments are a gift you give to someone else. And everyone likes presents. Get good at being sincere in your compliments as well as unique, whenever possible.

Compliments affect our self-perception profoundly. I can put on a shirt that I consider my least interesting shirt, that I wear because I don't want to get one of my favorite shirts dirty, and then someone will say, "I really like that shirt," and now suddenly I like the shirt a whole lot more. (By bizarre coincidence, as I sat in Starbucks typing this, a complete stranger said to me, "Nice shirt.")

People love compliments even when they aren't that believable. Because deep in their hearts, they *want* to believe them. It is the easiest and fastest way to make someone feel good about themselves (the prime directive).

Compliments are even more effective when they're unexpected. There are times when we expect them, even hope for them. But when someone sneaks up on us and surprises us by telling us something positive about ourselves, we feel a special glow. It can be even more unexpected if it is about something we don't necessarily believe about ourselves, or imagine is true.

However, telling a woman she looks sexy is generally a venture into creepytown. But if a woman tells a man he looks sexy in the suit he's wearing, she will get some big bonus points. Most likely, he's wearing the suit to look good, stylish even. But sexy? Now we're talking!

Giving compliments is an act of generosity. Here's a real-life example. I was riding in an elevator one night and two young women entered, and one was chatting away to her friend when she suddenly burped. I think she surprised herself, and she turned to me and said, "Excuse me. I am so sorry!" Then she added, "That was so un-feminine!"

I smiled and said, "Don't worry, you have more than enough femininity —you can get away with it."

And she smiled, delighted, and said, "That's so sweet. Thank you!"

Why did that happen that way? Simply because I was well practiced at talking to strangers and crafting compliments on the fly. My brain doesn't short-circuit, and I say something nice, and often unique, spontaneously.

When you are confident, you naturally want to make people feel good about themselves. Few things work as well as compliments. Be generous with them.

When preparing an introductory line, you can embed a compliment and jumpstart a positive exchange. Some examples:

"Hi, I'm Fred, I would really like to meet you."

"You look so familiar. Could I be lucky enough to already know you?"

"You seem very interesting, even from across the room."

Get the idea? Your goal is to say something that hopefully will make that person feel good about themselves, ideally in a way they don't expect. That means a well-crafted compliment of some kind. If you are not good at thinking of those, then all the more reason to practice.

You may even freak people out when you start saying something nice, since they've not heard much from you at all. That's a good thing. Roll with it. Expect nothing in return, though. That's not why you're doing it. You are being generous of spirit, the voice of upliftment, and that is its own reward.

When you start to do this, you will learn what I mean. To put a smile on someone's face, or just to know that you did something without expecting anything in return, becomes a precious gift you give yourself as well as them.

The Throwaway Compliment

One of the first Boldness Exercises you'll be practicing is what I call the throwaway compliment. That's when you offer a compliment to someone expecting nothing in return, not even a continuation of the conversation. I continue to be amazed at how receptive people are to a casual compliment when you clearly have no ulterior motive for saying it. (No agenda, remember?)

You brighten their day and your own. Why? Because it's an act of pure generosity, and once you learn in life the joy of generosity, it becomes more and more pointless to be stingy with positive words.

The steps are simple: notice something about someone, give them a compliment, and then walk away. That way they know you weren't using it as a way into a conversation. It was a total drive-by compliment. Like being Santa with positive words.

Even more important is to do it with people you know. In fact, that's where the Boldness Exercise starts. Go up to someone you know and just give them a random compliment. Also, when it comes to strangers, resist the urge to only compliment really attractive people or people you think are interesting. Be agnostic, ecumenical. Aim wide to get good at it. Lower the stakes emotionally for yourself. You'll be very surprised how appreciated it is by people who don't get compliments all the time. You may even think at first that what you are saying is not even believable. Go for it anyway. You'll be amazed at how they will believe you.

I now take it one step further. I pick the thing that actually bothers me about the person—their voice, their purple hair, their mismatched clothing—and I force myself to come up with a compliment about it. And two things happen: one, the person is highly appreciative, and two, suddenly the thing doesn't bother me anymore and my judgment about them is reversed. This is a little advanced because it takes some creativity, but I'm going to get you to try it eventually.

I've told people that their hair looked amazing when I thought it looked bizarre, and they were thrilled to hear it. Even goth people—whose clothing premise seems to be deliberately unattractive—want to know that they achieved the right appearance. You could say, "That's totally goth. You own that look." They'll look at you like you're joking with them, maybe, but do it sincerely, and smile. Not clownishly, but amiably.

I once told a friend who didn't like her nose, which was kind of big, that it was her nose that made her uniquely beautiful. She blushed. I told another friend, who always dresses so fashionably that most people think he overdoes it, that I don't know where he finds the time to shop for all these unique things. Instead of making fun of him (as old Fred would have), I made him feel like his effort was worth it. Why not make people feel good about themselves? Do we have to cut everyone down to size? Let other people do that. Not you.

I remember the lead character Buddy in the movie *Elf* telling this woman, "You are just as pretty as a postcard." Now, Buddy of course wasn't hitting on her. It was a genuine compliment, sweet and unassuming. And of course, the woman clearly felt wonderful. I know, it's a movie and people are acting, but I think you should be emulating Buddy, complimenting people all the time with no agenda, no ulterior motive.

Remember, these positive words stick with people, just like the negative ones do. You'll feel good doing it too. I promise you.

And that's perhaps the most interesting shift to observe. When you don't pursue the conversation any further, just offer up a throwaway compliment, their basic human cautiousness melts away because they see that you have no ulterior motive. It often stuns them into silence, but also boosts their faith in humanity in a subtle way. You can tell by the way their face softens that you got to them, you tagged them with a positive charge. Occasionally a real conversation ensues. Either way, you made it a better world.

Power Tool #5: Adding to Yes

This concept may be hard to grasp on the first pass, so I'm going to explain it in detail, starting with where I learned it, which was while studying improvisational comedy.

The best speaking training I ever got was in improv comedy classes. Not only are the basic principles of improv the same as what I'm training you to do with the PRIDE Method, the classes are a tremendous amount of fun. I've met some amazing people in the classes, some whom are still my friends twenty years later. Almost every city offers these classes.

The classes also apply the principle of Dosage brilliantly. The classes start you off very simply, using nonverbal exercises. They build gradually, step by step, exercise by exercise, until one day you suddenly can walk on a stage and create a scene with other performers out of thin air, without a script or even a plan.

One of the ironclad rules of improv comedy is this: when you are building a scene and it's your turn to speak or do an action, you are always adding positively to something. You never negate anything that has already been presented. That principle is called "Saying yes, and…"

For example, you can be creating a scene with another player, and she starts the scene by saying, "Here we are in sunny Central Park." You would then add something like, "*Yes, and* we're trying to find where we can go on a boat ride." You *wouldn't* say, "No, actually it's starting to rain." It throws the other person off, and it erases the foundation that was starting to be laid, because she said, "sunny Central Park." It essentially stops the scene in its tracks because you negated the information. Make sense?

It's exactly the same with conversation. The easiest way to build an interaction is by always adding something, not reversing the direction or negating what someone has just said. That way, the conversation gains momentum instead of screeching to a halt.

I think *adding to yes* is a great rule to apply to your whole life. But let's start with conversation. By starting your response with "Yes," you trick yourself into saying something positive. I recommend saying the "Yes, and…" out loud until you find yourself not needing to, until it becomes a reflex not to negate what someone is saying.

One of the traps of conversation many people fall into is contradicting someone with their superior knowledge. I talk about this later in the chapter on What Not to Do, but can you see how it negates what someone has said? Conversation is not a contest, unless proving how smart you are feels like a win (it's actually a loss, but more on that later).

Adding to Yes applies to actions as well as conversations. Bold people very often succeed because they are going along with the flow of something and adding to it. Very seldom are they reversing the direction of the action. It's much easier to take advantage of the direction something is already going, and then take a bolder step in that direction.

Power Tool #6: Saying the Unexpected

When we hear something we're expecting someone to say, we don't store it deep in our memory. What we do remember are unusual or unexpected things. This is how you can become memorable easily.

The first words you say to someone are not necessarily critical, but there are certainly ways to blow it. The first rule is, of course, to be simple and be courteous. But as you become more comfortable and trust yourself a bit more, then it's time to try to be a little bit unique. This is what will be happening in the second level of the Boldness Exercises.

Once you feel you are past the first stage of training, try saying something to a stranger that is not what they might expect you to say. For example, an attractive woman might be used to hearing about how beautiful she is. A very tall man will expect a height comment ("How's the air up there?").

So, go a different way. That doesn't mean go negative, and it doesn't mean trying to be witty, funny, or anything where you're trying to impress them. This is a social entryway, so it can't be intimidating or off-putting. Instead, you might comment on their clothing, or their car, or their choice of sandwich. Or even something about their attitude, like, "You seem to be a very confident person" or "Your smile is very infectious."

Or say something about the day, or the immediate environment. "Excuse me, but do you recognize the song that's playing? I can't place it and I don't know how to work Shazam."

The person may end up whipping out their phone and using Shazam to tell you what the song is. Remember, it's just an exercise, and you're flexing your wings a bit more. The conversation doesn't have to go further. But you may end up spending the next ten minutes talking about The Weeknd or Steely Dan.

Do I have to remind you that weird doesn't work? I'm hoping you have a sense of that, but some people don't. It's OK for you to *be* weird and quirky. I love that kind of person. But just realize and accept that you will appeal to a narrower spectrum of people. Unleashing your full weirdness is best saved for your own tribe, however large or small it might be.

If you want the skills to move between tribes, then you need to be aware of the rituals and behaviors of other tribes. Young entrepreneurs will have entirely different interests than actors and musicians, and devout Christians are unlikely to want to hear about your epic sexual adventures. Know your audience and know how to gauge them, and you will eventually speak several "tribal languages."

I'm not saying become a total chameleon, which in essence is losing your identity rather than shaping and expanding it. I'm saying choose how much to reveal about yourself and adapt with the goal in mind to be able to talk to anyone. At your best, you will still remain yourself while adapting to each audience. Especially with the Boldness Exercises, don't feel like you're sacrificing your integrity or your personality to test out new modes of communication. Just go with them to see how they feel, like trying on a new outfit you wouldn't normally wear.

To be memorable, get good at saying something positive and unexpected. Bold people are always memorable.

Here is one of the most unexpected things you can express: appreciation. We all are fairly terrible at expressing appreciation, and it is one of the most powerful messages you can give someone. It's memorable in large part because people seldom expect it. (A sad indictment of our society, but I can't fix that in this book. Maybe the next one.) Not that people don't want appreciation. They love it. You love it. I love it. But we're incredibly stingy with our appreciation. Change that.

I make a conscious effort to do it more. As a boss, it's essential; as a partner in a relationship, it's magical. As a human being, it's memorable because it is both generous and exceptional.

Once you realize how many situations present themselves when you can do this, you'll start to revel in the reactions you get. Thanking someone for being courteous or considerate will be both well received and likely to start a conversation. Letting someone close to you know that you appreciate what they do for you is an extremely loving gesture. It teaches them to do it too. Don't hesitate to express appreciation at every turn.

Power Tool #7: Employing the Power of Suspense

If you haven't noticed, every good story has suspense. In all good storytelling, something is always held back. The author doesn't tell you everything all at once. It's the same thing in conversation. Use suspense by not giving in to the urge to immediately roll out a whole story. Keep the listener wanting to hear more.

In our desperate need to be interesting, we often tell every detail, sometimes tipping into oversharing. Instead, dangle some interesting morsels and pique their interest without satisfying it. You know it works on you in books, TV, and movies. It's a basic principle of storytelling, and it works on everyone.

You could be telling someone about your trip to Africa. You would start by telling them where you went, and how exciting it was, and then you might say, "And the best part was the tour guide, who on the third day outdid himself and showed us something almost no one gets to see on safari. But tell me what's going on with you!" And you flip the conversation back to them, leaving them curious about the tour guide. Maybe later in the conversation, they will ask about the amazing thing he did. Or not, which is just as important, which means they weren't that interested. You definitely want to know that. You don't want to be babbling about your great adventures to people who don't care.

By combining the Power Tool of Asking Questions with the Power Tool of Suspense, you will seem more interested in them, which makes you even more interesting, with the suspense thrown in. For example, you could go on and give a full description of what you do for a living, what your job entails, who your clients are, and all that. Or you could say, "I work in an esoteric part of the communication field, but I'm more interested in what you do." See? You teased with a bit about yourself, and then you said you were more interested in who they were than talking about yourself. Wow. You really *are* in communication!

As always, don't expect everyone to care. In fact, it's a good gauge of a person when you ask them a series of questions about themselves and they never respond by asking questions in return. It's kind of telling how self-absorbed they are. Or maybe they're just shy or socially unskilled. Give them the benefit of the doubt. But don't blame yourself. And then break away. Who knows, later on they may come up to find out what you deliberately didn't tell them. How interesting would that be?

CHAPTER 11

EXERCISING YOUR IMAGINATION

n the Introduction, I said to you: **boldness is self-confidence in action. By** that I mean that bold people actively *pursue* things in the real world. But I also mean that bold people *impact* the world through their actions. Although much of my focus in the Boldness Exercises is about meeting people, cultivating boldness goes far beyond that in impact, both on yourself and the world around you. I would venture to say that it is bold individuals who make all the difference in the world. If Dr. Martin Luther King, Jr. didn't believe that he could attract thousands of people to Washington, DC for a civil rights rally, the world would not know his "I Have a Dream" speech. If Jonas Salk just decided to remain a general physician instead of relentlessly seeking a polio vaccine, how many more millions would have been afflicted? The list goes on, from Moses to Elon Musk. To you.

Bold people make a difference. Or at least they try. Are you going to change the world? Maybe. Who's to say you won't? But I know you can have a much greater impact on the world than if you just spent the rest of your life nestled in your comfort zone.

I want you to build boldness within yourself so you can turn your superpower on and feel what it is like to truly make a difference, whether it is in one person's life or solving world hunger. I want that to be up to you, with the tools to make whatever it is possible.

We're one chapter away from the Boldness Exercises now. You've gone through the steps of the PRIDE Method in depth, you've learned the Guiding Principles, you have your arsenal of Social Skills and Power Tools. In this chapter, we're going to do a few mental exercises—exercises of the imagination—to prepare you for bold action in the real world. But always keep in mind that they are training. You may get a real-world result sometimes, but the point is to develop bold skills and new neural pathways. So, let's start with an exercise in imagination.

YOUR LISTS

Which famous people would you like to meet?

The president? Oprah Winfrey? Drake? Ryan Reynolds? Beyoncé? Jay Z? Leonardo DiCaprio? Matt Damon? Bill Gates? Elon Musk?

Journal Entry #6: Your Fantasy List

Take a few minutes and make a list of anyone you would want to meet yet consider it impossible or at least incredibly unlikely to ever happen. It doesn't matter how famous. List at least five, but really let your imagination run wild. The only requirement is they have to be alive. Here's mine:

1. Bruce Springsteen
2. Bill Clinton
3. Jay Leno

4. Pope John Paul
5. Steven Spielberg
6. Meryl Streep
7. Joni Mitchell
8. Bill Murray
9. Tim Ferriss
10. Michael Connelly

Go to your journal and start creating your Fantasy List. Add to it whenever you think of someone new.

Now look at your list and realize this: they are all just people. They talk to other people all the time. Strangers, family, friends. So, it is not absolutely impossible for you to be one of those people they talk to. I know that you can think of a thousand reasons why it couldn't happen, but those are just excuses and rationalizations.

Sure, you could say, "I live on the South Pole and never leave. Meeting any one of those people would be impossible for me." OK, you win. Wait, no you don't. You could contact their agent or manager and say that you would be happy to give them a personal tour of your research facility if they ever find themselves in Antarctica. Suddenly, not impossible. Just unlikely. Like a million other things that happen to people all the time.

Journal Entry #7: Your Realistic Encounters List

Now make another list—a more realistic one—of whom you would like to meet in the next month. Is it your boss's boss? Is it that attractive person in accounting? Is it the neighbor three doors down? Your local mayor? The coach of your city's football team? Put anyone on the list that you have a desire to meet that also seems possible to you.

Go to your journal and make your Realistic Encounters List.

The purpose of these lists is for you to clearly see that there is a substantial gap between who you know and who you would like to know. There's nothing wrong with that. We all have those, but step by step you are going to start doing something about that. Boldness is going to close those gaps, one by one.

(And here's a little secret: I've already met five of the people on my Fantasy List. And I intend to meet every one of them eventually.)

Now, onto another crucial list.

Journal Entry #8: Your Dream Life List

Here I want you to list what you consider goals for your dream life. Who do you want to become? What do you want to achieve? What's on your bucket list? For the moment, I want you to let go of how long something might take or how much money would be required. They can be fanciful, be a one-time thing or take a lifetime, but I want you to stay in the range of what's possible. And they can be deeply personal as well.

Here are a variety of examples:

1. Meeting a life partner
2. Being a CEO
3. Creating a charitable foundation
4. Living in Europe for a month

5. Skydiving

6. Learning salsa dancing

7. Swimming with sharks

8. Opening a restaurant

9. Healing a relationship with a family member

To create the life you want, it is important to know what that life includes, and what that life looks like, and what experiences you want to have. Remember Insight #4 here, which is that you are the only one you need permission from to live that life. Fantasize it. Imagine it. Then let it pull you.

Go to your journal and make your Dream Life List.

YOUR DAILY INCANTATION

This step is a reprogramming exercise. The messages we tell ourselves every day about ourselves have the ability to shape our future. In fact, that is literally the story of your life. Therefore, I want you to craft a message that you tell yourself that reprograms you. I call it an incantation because I want you to repeat it every day exactly the same way. You need to make it a simple one, something that goes like this: "I love meeting new people. I look forward to it." Say it three times. Say it like you mean it. Like it's already true.

I use the word "incantation" because it has a specific meaning, which is "words used to summon a spirit." The spirit we are summoning is yours. Your full, true, unfiltered, uninhibited self. I want you to say it like you really, really mean it. Say it to yourself in the mirror. Write it to be exactly what you want to say, and it must describe an aspect of the person you most want to become. This may be a little scary. It may take you a little while to have the courage to say it out loud, even alone. Because this is you letting go of who you are, to discover who you might become.

This may seem weird to you—so what? Do it anyway for a week. It won't kill you, and no one is watching. Remember, if you want different results, do something different. For the best results, write the incantation on a sticky note and tape it to your bathroom mirror so that you start your day saying it. If you do it for a week and you still think it's stupid, maybe you need to go somewhere where people can't hear and shout it a few times so that you really feel it, and attach some emotion to it.

Also, these are not to be confused with affirmations like, "I'm going to make a million dollars this year." That's something else entirely. Your incantation is about reprogramming a negative thought into a positive one.

Journal Entry #9: Incantations

Don't forget to write your daily incantation in your journal. You'll want a record of it. Start with one incantation. But soon you are going to want to do more. One for every area that you want to change, every aspect of your life that needs a different story, a different mindset, a different daily message. I do it all the time, with all sorts of things at this point, even small, seemingly insignificant changes I want to bring about in myself. It's remarkably effective.

For example, I recently started exercising again heavily, and my trainer explained to me how important it was to stretch after a workout. But I really disliked stretching and that's what I told myself. Then I decided to rewrite my belief. I started saying to myself, "I love stretching. It's my favorite part of the whole workout."

You know what happened? Within a week, I started to like doing them. I actually started to look forward to stretching. And then I started to feel better and looser the next day because of those stretches. Then I added more stretches. That felt better too. And now, guess what? Stretching *is* my favorite part of the workout. New neural pathways were created. Code was rewritten.

OK, so we human beings are a little nuts, but incantations work. It's just simple reprogramming. That's what you're going to do with your daily incantations. Commit to it for a week. You'll surprise yourself with how fast it will change you. Then stick with it. Make it true. Add more of them.

Go to your journal and list all the incantations you create over time. You should also be adding them as sticky notes on your mirror.

CRINGEWORTHY MOMENTS

I hope you can see by now that I have had plenty of memories of either shy behavior or a lack of boldness that torment me when I recall them. I also have many times where I said or did the wrong thing because I was anxious, awkward, and under-confident. I call them my *cringeworthy moments*. You undoubtedly have some as well.

These are moments in your life where you still cringe whenever you think about them, either because you were socially inept or you missed an opportunity that would have led to something wonderful. I'm going to attempt to take some of the sting out of them, put them in the right context, and in the end drastically reduce their number in your future. Here's how we do it.

Journal Entry #10: My Cringeworthy Moments

I want you to start making a list of your own painful incidents. This goes in your journal. Every time you recall one, write it down in the My Cringeworthy Moments section. If you really want to highlight them, post them on my blog site and read other people's so that you can see that you are not alone. The truth is, we all have some of these moments, but some of us react better than others to them and learn from them, and the rest of us beat ourselves up until the memory fades. Which may be never.

It's very important to write these experiences down. When you make the entry, add what you could have said or done, or wished you'd done or said instead. If you can, write what you think you missed out on because of your inaction. Be specific and give some detail, because no one's going to read it but you, but I seriously want you to stop burying these memories.

It will also motivate you to stop doing things like these and develop the skills to act with social ease and boldness. In fact, they are the pavestones to your path to boldness. Bring them right to the painful reminder level because that's what will light the fire for your self-improvement. We don't want to waste energy regretting the past because, as I said, it's only a failure if you don't learn something. This turns them into motivation.

If you are suppressing some of the memories because they hurt too much, I completely understand. But those may be the most important ones to work through.

List any of those Cringeworthy Moments you can remember now in your journal.

CHANGING
WHAT SOMETHING MEANS

One of the strongest habits for your personal development and general happiness is the ability to reset yourself. When you feel bogged down, depressed, frustrated, or disappointed, you need to stop and consciously make an effort to shift your mood or your state. I call it "hitting the refresh button." Clear out all those temporary files that are clogging your brain and preventing you from seeing what is actually true.

Add this practice to your tool kit. It's a simple reminder that the past needs to be learned from and left behind so you can make progress. Easy? No. But you have to ask why you're hanging onto those feelings, those regrets, or that crappy mood. What's in it for you? Is it helping? I doubt it, and so should you.

Empty the trash. Clear out that clutter of worthless memories and erroneous scripts. Fill yourself with discoveries, joy, mystery, and audacious moments of love, passion, and purpose.

One of the most powerful ways to reset yourself is to change the meaning of something. There is no such thing as an absolute fact. We interpret everything that happens to us and become attached to that specific meaning. Often that interpretation is not just wrong but is preventing our own happiness and progress.

That's why the first essential step toward becoming bold is to let go of *barrier beliefs* that are doing you no good. The second essential step is to let go of *interpretations of your experiences* that are doing you no good. How do you do that? Simply by asking this very powerful question:

"What *else* could this mean?"

I'll give you an example. You see someone talking with a coworker, and they're both glancing at you and then they start laughing and turn away. You could easily interpret that exchange as them having a joke at your expense. And yet, do you know this for a fact? Absolutely not. It's a suspicion, at best. (I've had this paranoid reaction plenty of times, so I know what I'm talking about.)

They could just as easily be retelling a time when you said something witty at the perfect moment. Or they could be reflecting on the fact that the boss thinks you are an exemplary employee, but he doesn't realize you spend half your day on Facebook. But your reaction is to resent them for the perceived slight. You don't confront them on it, you just play it over and over in your head, getting more resentful with every replay.

The bold person, on the other hand, walks right up and says, "OK, let me in on the joke. Unless I am the joke, in which case you need to thank me for giving you a laugh. A little appreciation is in order."

How powerful would that feel? They will be impressed, if not awed and a bit embarrassed if they were indeed mocking you.

How often have you felt hurt or offended by something someone said, or *might* have said, about you, only to discover later that was not what they meant, or not what they even said? Or maybe you observed something and ascribed a meaning to it, only to discover it meant something else entirely? We all do it. And it drains our energy and diminishes our joy.

What resolves this behavioral trap is to simply consider the possibility that you might be wrong in your assumption. Call it the benefit of the doubt or optimism but, in reality, it's just the truth. Because there is no way that your assumptions are always 100 percent accurate. In fact, many times we jump to conclusions based on shreds of evidence and fill in the missing facts. We suspect people are talking about us, saying something bad or critical, when they are not even talking about us at all.

We all see things through our prism of our biases and fears. As one person said to me, there are always three sides to every story: yours, mine, and the truth. Now there's some truth!

And hey, maybe they were talking about you, maybe even in a negative way. So what? Are they right about you? Does it matter? This also brings up another trap. We think we need to be perfect, and so any of our quirks and foibles that people might be laughing at are painful to us. When in reality they love us for those quirks, even though they may make fun of them, and they love us even more when we laugh along with them. No one is perfect. Don't fall into the resentment trap.

The Resentment Trap

One of the most profound observations I've ever heard is this:
"Resentment is like drinking poison hoping the other person dies."
We resent people and they don't care (and maybe don't even know).
It's eating us alive, taking away our joy, making us miserable, and the other person is going on like nothing happened. I know people who are still carrying resentment from an incident twenty years earlier. Amazingly, the other person still hasn't died, even though the resentful person keeps chugging that poison.

Why create negative feelings in yourself? It's more than just a waste of calories. It's self-defeating. Even if other people are saying bad things about you, they most likely don't give a tinker's damn if you resent them for it.

This alternative course of action is powerful: **change what something means!**

There is often a huge difference between what someone said and how you decide to interpret it. There is also very often a huge difference between what someone's true motivation is for doing something and the motivation we ascribe to it.

What do I mean by this exactly? Let me give you a simple example. You're driving, and someone cuts you off. Your most predictable reaction is "What a freaking jerk!" and you may even invest some negative emotional energy by flipping the person off or pounding your steering wheel and swearing.

But do you really KNOW that person is a jerk? Could it not also be that they were so late for work that they might get fired? Or that the woman of their dreams was at the airport and all they could think about was getting there as fast as possible? Or maybe their bladder is about to explode, and they need a restroom fast. I could give you twenty reasons why someone would cut you off and you would gladly let them do it.

But what did you do? You assumed the worst and let all sorts of anger hormones squirt into your bloodstream. You laid on your horn, and you let it bother you for the next five minutes or two hours. How much time did it really cost you? One second? Three? Are you telling me that you are so time efficient that when someone steals three seconds from you that the loss is enraging?

Don't forget, the person who cut you off is fine. Even after you flipped him off.

So, when you find yourself having a negative reaction and the only person being damaged is you, change what that thing means. By the way, I give total credit to Tony Robbins for this insight. It is one of his most powerful and profoundly influential teachings on how to change the mental state you're in. Changing what something means releases you from the negative grip an experience has on you. It's liberating and will make you a happier person.

So, don't get attached to negative interpretations. You're the one who benefits from giving the benefit of the doubt. Later, you'll do a specific Boldness Exercise about this, but for now it is about changing your state of mind. I want you to see what's possible, so let's make it personal.

Journal Entry #11: Meanings I Could Change

Take a few moments and think of two or three experiences that really bothered you, and probably still bother you. They could be very significant in your life or only mildly so. Write them down and then come up with at least two alternative meanings.

Start with the fact, and then your interpretation, and then add a new meaning or two.

For example:

Fact: My brother owes me a lot of money and never brings it up.

Interpretation: He only cares about himself.

Alternate meaning one: He's embarrassed that he's mismanaged his money so badly that he can't talk to me about it, because I am so much wiser with my finances.

Alternate meaning two: This is a weakness of his, and I still love him in spite of this, and I need to find a way to communicate about the problem.

Do you see how a bold move could result from your two alternative meanings?

List at least three meanings you could change now in your journal.

PART IV

THE BOLDNESS
EXERCISES

CHAPTER 12

THE BOLDNESS EXERCISES: OVERVIEW

"Lack of fear is not courage.
Lack of fear is mental illness."
—Unknown

CONQUERING FEAR IS EXHILARATING

Becoming bold is going to involve facing down your fears. Most people do not deliberately seek to conquer their fears. Instead, they use fear as a guide to what to avoid. But, when you actually face those fears and defeat them, it's thrilling. It starts to change your definition of yourself.

These do not have to be huge victories. A simple conversation or seizing a little opportunity is very gratifying and reinforces boldness. Boldness isn't so much about a lack of fear, as it is about facing down your fear and discovering something wonderful on the other side.

When I visited New Zealand several years ago, I went to the Kawarau River Bridge, where bungee jumping was invented. I have no fear of heights, so I was raring to go. But the girl who was in front of me in line, once she got the gear attached to her legs and was standing on the launch platform, started bawling her eyes out and saying, "I can't do it! I'm terrified of heights! I don't know why I thought I could do it! You have to push me!"

She was asking the bungee crewman to give her a push. In typical New Zealander fashion, he replied, "I'm not gonna push you, love. You can stand here all day if you want. Or you can step down. Or you can jump. It's all up to you. But I'm not gonna push you."

At that point I would have bet a thousand dollars that she was going to step back down. But she stood there, trembling, tears streaming down her face as she stared at the river below. Then, after twenty minutes, she jumped. I was shocked. But what was even more surprising was that after they disconnected her from the cord and brought her back to shore, she came running back up to do it again!

Even though I didn't know her, I was so proud of her because she stayed right in her fear, bathed in her terror, until she beat it. And she was rewarded for it because she learned two amazing lessons that day. She vocalized the first one when she was back on the bridge. "If that was so much fun," she said, panting with excitement, "and I was so scared of it until I did it, why would I ever be scared of anything ever again?!?!"

She had paved a new neural pathway deep and wide with that big bold move.

She also learned something else a little more subtle, but just as profound, and that's this: she didn't actually have to jump. All she had to do was lean ten degrees forward, and then everything happened on its own. In other words, all she had to do was commit and not give herself a way out, a way back to her comfort zone, and the joy of powering through her fear and finding some real enjoyment was waiting right there for her.

That's how I want you to think about these Boldness Exercises. Put yourself in a position where you are committed and there is no way back to your comfort zone. Lean ten degrees forward and discover what gifts lie on the other side.

Imagine if she hadn't jumped. If she had just climbed down and given up. How long would she regret that? I'm guessing the rest of her life. Now it's your turn to jump.

THIS IS TRAINING

The design of the Boldness Exercises in the next chapters is to move you gradually upward in boldness, each level creating a foundation for the next. This system is as simple and methodical as learning to run a marathon. You would not start training for a marathon by running 26.2 miles the first time out. You wouldn't even do five miles on your first run because you'd likely injure yourself, perhaps permanently, but most certainly you'd delay your progress. Instead, you would start with short runs, gradually increasing in duration and intensity. Then within a few months you'd be ready for the full marathon. Then you'd start improving your technique and your time.

The parallel is exact. As you work on your boldness, you need to pace yourself, training consistently, working your way up gradually and steadily to the level you want to be, and not set yourself back with injuries along the way. Becoming bold isn't a switch you're going to flip. It's an evolutionary process with many victories along the way.

You're going to make entries into your journal celebrating these moments so that you can look back in a month or two and see how shy or hesitant you were. You will most likely laugh at the situations where you held yourself back, as they will have become child's play to you. A year from now, you won't even believe the difference. Three years from now, you'll just be wincing at all those daunting and painful situations that once plagued you. Or maybe you'll just be laughing because they are no longer part of you, and don't haunt you at all.

WHAT TO EXPECT

You need to prepare yourself mentally for what can occur during the Boldness Exercises. These are some of the possibilities of what could happen:

- People won't say hi back.
- People may think you're strange.
- People may act uncomfortable.
- People may respond rudely.
- People won't respond at all.

And these responses are most likely what will freak you out. Most people can't take even a single rejection. We're like the opposite of a professional gambler, who takes losses in stride, believing that winning is as close as the next card. But these are Boldness Exercises. They are designed to soften the blow, so to speak, so you can build up your strength, just like a boxer in training wears a helmet and fat gloves so he learns not to flinch and to take the punches in stride.

Right now, you take these kinds of things very personally, and then you rationalize why that person doesn't merit a conversation. I know the grip fear of rejection has on you. I'm going to loosen that grip, one day, one exercise, one hello at a time.

Because what will feed you and give you positive reinforcement is a nice, healthy win, just like the gambler. Your win will be a broad smile from someone, an expression of genuine appreciation from a stranger, or perhaps even a delightful exchange going beyond just superficial banter to expressing who you are or allowing someone to express who they are. Then you'll develop a taste for it and eventually an immunity to rejection.

Like all immunizations, it will take time, and you may not always feel great right after the shot!

That's why I want you to go into many of the Boldness Exercises expecting failure, expecting rejection, so that everything positive you get will be a bonus, and anything negative is what you were already anticipating.

I don't expect you will ever love rejection. The professional gambler doesn't like losing. He just doesn't let it take the wind out of his sails, nor does he let the losses of a day keep him from getting up the next day and going at it again. Sure, he may call it quits for the day, but only after many attempts.

Entrepreneurs behave the same way. Failures are part of the training, part of the process of refining their businesses. Both the entrepreneur and the gambler know that life is a numbers game. A win is coming sooner or later, if they can just keep at it. Unlike the gambler, you have nothing to lose by playing. And you're going to get to the point where you are winning so much that you won't even feel the occasional rejection, and maybe you'll even laugh at it.

So, let the training begin!

CHAPTER 13

EXERCISES: LEVEL 1

H ere is how I want you to be thinking about this chapter.

First of all, remember that these are *exercises*. They are designed to get you to flex and develop new muscles, the atrophied side of your social development. They are crafted to gradually shake something loose in you, to slowly unhinge you from that narrow frame in which you've defined yourself. They are not meant to be radical changes in your life or your lifestyle. The approach and the results will be gradual and cumulative, just like any form of exercise.

The intention is for you to consciously experience your reaction and other people's when you do each exercise. In particular, I want you to experience the lack of real consequence to these actions, despite the bizarreness of some of them, and to make special note of the fear that they might generate in you.

These are the rules to follow when doing Boldness Exercises:

1. *Work at a pace appropriate for you.* Everyone is different. You may leap through the first and second levels in a week or stay at Level 1 for a month. You alone know that boundary, so you will have to fashion your exercise pace based on your own Dosage. They are designed so the average person could complete them in ninety days, but you may take twice as long. So what? The reward will be huge, affecting the rest of your life.

2. *Expect to feel uncomfortable.* You will be Prepared, and attempting to rRelax, but this will not be a miraculous transformation. Embrace the discomfort. If you are deliberately aiming for it, you won't be as freaked out. Ideally, you don't want your mouth dry, your armpits wet, your tongue tied and your mind unraveling. You don't want the discomfort to paralyze you. If it does, start slower. But don't go too easy on yourself. Discomfort, not paralysis, is the goal.

3. *Expect a negative response.* Or no response at all. What? Yes, the strategy is you are setting yourself up for deliberate failure in many of the exercises. This eliminates any possibility of disappointment.

4. *Pick a person who is not crucial to you meeting.* If the specific exercise requires you to interact with someone and you perceive the stakes to be high, then it will be more difficult. Remember, we're trying to keep the Dosage low. For example, if one of your goals is to be comfortable striking up a conversation with a person that you find appealing, the target of your exercise will be to strike up a conversation with a different person, someone you will be just fine with if you had never met them.

5. *Don't let yourself off the hook.* If you are frozen with fear attempting one Boldness Exercise, pick a different one. But stay

committed for as long as it takes to act at least once a day. If you miss one day, get right back on schedule the next day.

6. *Return to the PRIDE Method steps.* If you find yourself frozen in your tracks somewhere during the exercise, it usually means you missed a step. Start over.

7. *Repeat each level until you feel comfortable moving up.* It's not a race or a competition. It's about expanding your comfort zone at a pace that doesn't set you back. Go back to the exercises in that level that made you most uncomfortable and repeat those.

8. *Once you move to the next exercise, that doesn't mean stop doing the previous ones.* You can add some of them to your daily activity, and most likely you'll want to. You may find yourself doing several different Boldness Exercises in a single day. Think of it exactly like physical exercises. You'd start with pushups, then add sit-ups, then lunges. The workout gets bigger as you broaden your skills and strength. Hopefully you'll sweat less than you would in the gym, but maybe not.

With each exercise, make an entry in your journal that day. The Appendix specifies all the detail you should include with each entry.

EXERCISE 1

Smile at five complete strangers.

One at a time, if I have to clarify.

This is learning to employ the first Power Tool. It could be to someone walking in your direction, or it could be someone stopped in the car next to you at a traffic light. Expect them not to smile back. (Rule #3.) They might think you're a bit crazy. But are you any crazier than a person running in place as they wait for the light to change so they can continue their jog? You're exercising too. Nothing crazy about that.

Examine how you feel when someone smiles back. And how you feel when they don't. Eventually you will have an insight into how truly harmless this is.

Do this five times each day until you feel ready to add the next exercise. Apply the PRIDE Method:

- Preparation: Brush your teeth. Smile in the mirror.
- Relaxing: Breathe. Play your theme song in your head.
- Insight: People tend to smile back at someone. It doesn't matter if they don't. We don't know their headspace. We are doing it as an act of pure positive generosity. Expecting nothing.
- Dosage: Minimum one smile to a stranger. (The goal is five, but feel free to do it all day.)
- Every Day Action: Don't let the day end without doing this. (Do it early.)

Pitfalls: Holding someone's gaze too long. Smiling like a crazy person. Invading someone's space. Cheating by smiling at someone you know. That's OK, of course, but the exercise is to smile at a complete stranger.

Journal your experience: With this and all the exercises, record the results of the day.

EXERCISE 2

Say one sentence to a stranger.

This may seem like a giant leap forward, but it's critical to break the verbal barrier. The Dosage is simple: one sentence. That sentence could be "Hi." This doesn't take a lot of Preparation. You are going to say something very simple. Remember the expectation, which is a negative response or no response at all. Anything beyond that is a bonus.

You are not asking them a question, just making a statement, an observation.

Now that we're leaping to verbal exercises, let's break down the PRIDE steps in more detail.

Preparation: Think of the exact thing you will say, that you could say to almost anyone, like, "I'm glad it stopped raining" or "Summer's almost here." Say it out loud, alone, until it feels natural. Because you want to make sure you say it audibly and it flows off your tongue. Say it five times if you have to. Do it in the mirror so you can see that you're smiling while you say it. Examples would be "It's such a nice day today" or "I love it when the elevator goes right to my floor without stopping."

Relaxing: The moment before you speak to someone, take two or three deep breaths. Center yourself. Shake off the tension. Start your theme song playing in your head. Do the vagus breath if you're feeling any anxiety.

Insight: You will not die, no matter what happens. This will be an insignificant moment in both your lives. The first few times you will likely mess this up, and that is part of it. You expect to. And it won't matter. If you were learning to juggle, wouldn't you expect to drop a ball a few times? I thought so. Same thing here.

Dosage: Control the amount of speaking you plan to do. If you intend to invite a response, have your own response prepared. If that is too much for you at the outset, prepare a simple observation that doesn't require further interaction, like, "The sky is so blue today" or "I think traffic is better today than usual." No exchange beyond that is necessary in this exercise.

Every Day Action: Once you start, you are going to do this every day. Your personal Dosage control will determine your minimum number of times, but it's going to be at least one. Do it early in the day so you can have a win, and maybe do it again. Or maybe stack up a bunch of rejections, just for the fun of it.

To summarize:

Preparation: Three possible opening lines—simple comments or observations.

Relaxing: Three deep breaths. (Add the vagus breath if necessary.)

Insight: You won't die. And you are expecting no response.

Dosage: Minimum one sentence to one stranger. Ideally do it until you have one total failure.

Every Day Action: Don't let the day end without doing this. (Do it early.)

Pitfalls: Starting a conversation you can't handle yet. Not smiling or making eye contact as you do the exercise.

EXERCISE 3

Ask a stranger a question.

Same as Exercise 2, except now you are going to ask a question instead of making a statement. Something that requires a simple response, like, "Yes" or "I agree." Something like, "How was your weekend?" or "What did you think of the Super Bowl?" Say it out loud, alone, until it feels natural. You're still going to break away after they respond. If the exchange goes further, run it out until you feel uncomfortable. That would be the bolder approach to the exercise.

Pitfalls: Not listening to the answer and not responding if necessary.

EXERCISE 4

Learn someone's name.

This is learning to employ the second Power Tool. This sounds simple, except that you know that it isn't. Because *learning* someone's name means you'll remember it the next time you see them. This could be someone you work with, if you're in a big office, or it could be the security guard you see every day, or the barista at your local coffee shop, or a waiter. Or someone you meet at a party, a seminar, or just someone you want to meet. This is not something you do with a passing stranger, unless it's a follow-up to a previous exercise. It may also be polite to offer your name first, then wait for them to respond with theirs.

Also, consider that neighbor you've never met, or that person you pass on your way to work or in your building, whose name you never learned. How about starting with them?

Preparation: Be ready to smile and make eye contact, and think of how exactly you are going to do it—either by offering your name first or by simply asking theirs. Have the exact line ready. When in doubt say, "Hi, I'm Fred. What's your name?"

Relaxing: Three deep breaths. Theme song. Vagus breath optional.

Insight: Most people like to hear their name. Most people are happy to tell you their name. (And will forget yours.)

Dosage: Learn and remember at least one name a day.

Every Day Action: Don't let the day end without doing this. (Do it early.)

Examples:

"Would you mind telling me your name?"

"I should know your name. What is it?"

"Hi, I'm Fred." If they don't say their name back, ask.

"I'm sorry, I don't know your name. I'm Fred."

Pitfalls: Having to ask a third time because you forgot their name. Not telling them your name. Getting tricky, like saying, "You're not Lisa, are you?" when you know they're not. That violates my "no scam approach" principle (we'll unpack this in Chapter 16, What Not to Do).

EXERCISE 5

Compliment a stranger.

In other words, make someone feel better about themselves, as in, the prime directive. This is a big step, because Preparation now happens right before you speak. It's going to require that you prepare something in your head when you see the person you want to offer a compliment to.

Remember and apply the rules about compliments in Chapter 10 (Power Tool #4). Make it easy on yourself at first. Don't go for something complex or wordy. And avoid physical attributes, for now. The perverse side of you will want to say something like, "Those are the biggest ears I've ever seen." Shut that voice down!

In this Boldness Exercise, you do not continue with the conversation. This is a drive-by, a throwaway compliment. You are making someone feel good about themselves, expecting nothing in return. So, break away after they respond. Or just be quiet. They will be a little bit surprised that you have no ulterior motive, no agenda. Big points for you.

Preparation: Choose the person, choose the thing about them you want to compliment, and then create the line in your head.

Relaxing: Take three deep breaths. Think your theme song. Adjust your body language.

Insight: You won't die. People tend to believe compliments and appreciate them from anyone, as long as they are not done in a creepy way. Remember, you are expecting nothing positive or significant in return.

Dosage: Minimum one compliment to one stranger.

Every Day Action: Don't let the day end without doing this. (Do it early.)

Pitfalls: Space invading (getting too close). Not smiling and making eye contact. Not breaking away and ending up in a dead-end exchange.

EXERCISE 6

Compliment a stranger that you have a specific negative judgment about.

This is a variation on the previous Boldness Exercise, with the obvious adjustment.

This should actually be a really easy exercise in one aspect, because you are running these judgments through your mind constantly as you observe people or listen to them. You know how this goes. You're standing there, looking at someone and defining them based on the fact that they are wearing a ball cap backward, or have a goatee, or an expensive purse. Or they're frowning. Or laughing loudly. Most of us do these judgments instantly and reflexively. That's the exact person I want you to compliment.

So ideally, you take the exact thing you are judging them about and fashion your compliment based on that. (I know. This suddenly makes it much harder.) When you offer a compliment to someone you actually have a negative judgment about, both of you are affected. The person is not expecting it, and you have reversed your negative judgment by making that person real instead of a biased caricature in your mind.

Imagine you see someone wearing all yellow and you think that's ridiculous, but instead you say, "That is a bold statement you're making. I love yellow!" You voiced the opposite of your judgment. And you know what? You won't die because you contradicted your pointless and most often inaccurate opinion. You'll actually feel better when you make that person feel better about themselves.

They may reveal themselves to you in an unexpected way because of it. Imagine if the person in yellow said, "Thank you so much for saying that. I've been struggling with depression and I decided to go extremely bright and colorful to snap myself out of it." Wouldn't that feel great to hear? Wouldn't that make them so very human to you? What a wonderful, unexpected gift you just gave that person, and yourself.

I'm telling you this because I have been bad at this most of my life, probably more than you will ever be. It feels safe to judge people silently, to have sneering opinions about people we don't know at all. But even as we retreat behind the bravado of being aloof or obnoxious, we feel the pain of disconnecting.

I have now become addicted to taking the time to notice whom I'm having a judgment about and then forcing myself to find something good to say to make them feel better about themselves. Anyone can tell a pretty girl she looks pretty, or a well-dressed man he looks sharp. But what about the man with the clearly anachronistic mustache? It's so easy to say to yourself, "Seriously, buddy? A waxed, curled mustache? Could you look more peculiar?"

This is the golden opportunity to go against your own warped grain and say, "Dude, that's an awesome 'stache." And he gives you a broad grin and you get to think, "Hey, he's a human being with feelings and pride and vanity, just like the rest of us." And suddenly the incessant judgment broadcast playing in your head shuts off for a few seconds, and you get to feel good about making someone feel good.

When you have taken the urge to judge someone and turned that into a unique compliment, then you will have made it over one of the biggest walls you've built around yourself.

That behavior is something I hope you get sharply attuned to—**the pain of disconnecting**—for within it is the root cause of our unhappiness. When we disconnect from others, whether to protect ourselves or to punish someone who made us feel embarrassed, or inadequate, or insignificant, we climb deeper inside our dark little shell, and it gets harder to find our way out. And eventually we believe the shell is the most important part of ourselves, that it *is* ourselves. When it is no more "ourselves" than an overcoat we might be wearing. Shed this shell, and happiness is right around the corner.

Preparation: See the person, listen to your judgment, reverse it to find a compliment about it, and prepare the exact line in your head. Make eye contact and smile.

Relaxing: Three deep breaths. Theme song. Adjust your body language. Vagus breath (quietly if you are in public).

Insight: You won't die. It's a rare person who doesn't like a compliment, and if they don't, they are in a negative headspace at the moment. It is not you. You're moving on.

Dosage: Minimum one judgment-reversing compliment to a stranger.

Every Day Action: Don't let the day end without doing this. (Do it early.) If you can't find a stranger, at least do it with someone you know.

Pitfalls: Coming up with a creepy compliment. Sounding fake. Using clichés. Space invading. Not breaking away. Not saying, "You're very welcome" if they say, "Thank you."

EXERCISE 7

Introduce yourself to a stranger.

This exercise can be an add-on to one of the previous exercises, once you feel less uncomfortable with them. (Notice I didn't say, "Once you feel comfortable with them." I don't want you to wait that long!) In its ideal form, the exercise is done in a situation where there are a number of people you don't know, and perhaps some that you do, such as a party or a meeting. It could even be with a new employee at your workplace.

You are going to approach the person and say, "Hi, I'm _____. I'd like to meet you."

Now, you can follow it with a compliment, or start with one and then introduce yourself. It works either way. And very likely you will shake hands, if you are a man. Women have to gauge the situation more closely and decide if it merits a handshake or if it is a more casual first encounter. I would lean toward a handshake in most situations.

You are not to proceed to the next batch of exercises until you can do this. This may freeze you in your tracks the first few times you set out to do it. Stay with it until you feel like you can be at least 50 percent relaxed as you do it.

You can still choose to break away after a quick exchange, but since you did introduce yourself, you might have to converse. Now you have to ask some questions. Listen to the answers. Remember their name. Don't break away abruptly, despite your nervousness. That would be a little rude. Have a sense of when you could gracefully break away, or just stay with the person until it becomes uncomfortable. (It's an exercise, remember? You're pushing to the point of failure.) That will be what you want to observe. How did that happen? What was the moment that caused it?

It's an easy breakaway. "Really nice to meet you." Smile. Shake hands, maybe. Walk away.

Preparation: Choose the person, then choose a simple, well-rehearsed introductory line. Nothing clever, witty, or sarcastic. Just something casually cordial. Make eye contact and smile. Come up with a potential compliment. Have your breakaway line ready.

Relaxing: Three deep breaths. Theme song. Dry your hand if you need to.

Insight: You won't die. You are aiming to fail, so anything else will be a bonus.

Dosage: One stranger. Three sentences minimum.

Every Day Action: Don't let the day end without doing this. If you have to go into a grocery store and do it, fine.

Pitfalls: Space invading. Breaking away too soon. Not following up with a question or two or a compliment, if called for. Forgetting their name.

EXERCISE 8

Meet people at an event where they will be wearing name tags.

This is an open-invitation environment where people can walk up to strangers, so you are going apply all the skills of the previous Boldness Exercises. You'll learn people's names, and say yours, so they don't have to look at your name tag. Then ask them something simple about themselves. Be careful not to start to babble or monologue, as that is the reflex when people in these groups meet.

Break away at a certain point, and then circle back to the person much later. Pay them a compliment, like saying that they were the most interesting person you met all night. (You can say this to more than one person, but don't say it five or six times!) Repeat this exercise with several people until you find your Dosage limit. Be sure to make everyone feel good about themselves.

EXERCISE 9

Use people's names for an entire day.

With everyone you encounter in any service capacity, use their name. Your coffee server, the waitress, the grocery checkout person, the security person in your building, absolutely everyone for the entire day. They should have a name tag, but if they don't, ask their name. Use it twice if you can. This is different as a Boldness Exercise because it's not just one action, but a series, taken whenever there is an opportunity. These are easy targets, and most other people don't use or even know these people's names, so you will be the uplifting voice in their day.

EXERCISE 10

Positive Judgment Day.

All day, with everyone you see—strangers, friends, coworkers—have a positive judgment in your head about them, and try not to couple it with a negative one. You will find this incredibly hard at first. You'll also notice how often you play a negative judgment in your head about someone and how comfortable you are doing it (since no one can hear you).

This doesn't take much Preparation, unless you are unable to think positive thoughts. This is more about gaining an insight about yourself and starting to reprogram that behavior. The Dosage is that we are not saying it out loud. Hopefully you don't need to relax too much to do this, unless you think people can read your mind. But it may even have a relaxing effect on you, and you will have a different hormonal response by being so much more positive than negative.

Because this is an all-day exercise, I want you to record as many of these positive judgments as possible.

Journal Entry #11: Positive Judgments

Keep track of these judgments in your journal. If you want something more immediate for this exercise, you can get a little notepad that you carry with you or use Evernote on your phone. Include the negative judgment that you may have started with. Do it for an entire day, and you'll amaze yourself, and not in a good way.

You will probably find it hard to keep up, there will be so many judgments. That guy who's driving too slowly, that woman with the big hair, the dude in the Speedo at the beach, the woman with the spider-web tattoos. With everyone you don't know that you've rendered a judgment about, try to remember and write it down, and hopefully in your mind you've flipped each one to a positive judgment.

Another trick, especially if you find yourself with an endless stream of judgments, is to wear a rubber band on your wrist and snap it against your skin every time you have a judgment. It will cue you to turn it into a positive judgment. By the end of the day, I'm willing to bet your wrist will hurt like hell!

You are going to repeat this exercise once a week for the first month, and then once a month thereafter. Then hopefully at the end of a year, you will have reduced the number of judgments, especially negative ones, drastically. (This exercise is not an Every Day Action, but I expect you to start noticing every day when you do have negative judgments, and watch them diminish over time.)

Also, if you do encounter the person and engage them in some way and they turn out to be different than you imagined, make a journal entry about that as well. Then calculate how often you were wrong.

> Write down every negative judgment you have about anyone for
> an entire day and change those judgments into positive judgments.
> Repeat this each week for a month, and then once every month
> for a year.

EXERCISE 11

Defuse a cringeworthy moment.

You need to unburden yourself of the humiliations you are carrying around. The best way to do that is to tell someone about them. Choose one of your cringeworthy moments, and tell someone, "Here is one of my most embarrassing/disappointing/ridiculously missed opportunities because I hesitated/was too shy/lacked social skills or sense."

Spill your guts to your friend. It will defuse the event, minimize it, or neutralize the cringe factor. Often, you'll find the other person has something equally embarrassing they need to release themselves from. Or they will just put yours in proper perspective. Sometimes they will laugh—not at you, but because they identify with the experience and the feeling.

It makes you human.

And it will set you free.

This also requires you to control the Dosage. Don't disgorge your worst moment to someone right out of the gate. Just pick one you can handle revealing. Eventually you are going to go through your entire list. Also, at this level you are not going back to the person with whom the moment actually occurred. That's for later. For this specific exercise, you're telling someone else.

Of course, don't feel like you have to confess to an actual crime, and make sure you are not hurting anyone by revealing your story. Better to endure the embarrassment and leave it unexpressed, in that case. I'm quite serious about this. Consider the effect on other people when you choose to reveal your innermost horrors. You've got plenty of them, so just pick ones that first do no harm.

RECOGNIZING YOUR PLATEAU

Some of the Boldness Exercises are going to be difficult at the start because, depending on your level of unboldness, you quite possibly have structured an existence where you limit your public encounters, and you seldom rub elbows with anyone you don't know well already, either at work or in your close social circle. That is going to change, and you're going to have to thrust yourself into new environments. And soon you'll want to.

The next step with all the exercises in Level 1 is to increase your Dosage, meaning do the exercise more than the minimum per day. Also, some of the exercises can be combined, but make sure they are completed. For example, you can compliment someone and then introduce yourself, but if you forget their name, you didn't really complete the exercise. Try again.

Your individual plateau can be gauged by how comfortable you feel doing these exercises. It may take you a month to get through Level 1 and be doing them at triple the Dosage, meaning multiple exercises multiple times a day. Or you may be ready for Level 2 in a week. Everyone is different. There will be a moment when you feel pulled to go to the next level. That's when you're ready. Your confidence is building, as is your communication skill level.

Keep in mind that these Boldness Exercises are giving you basic social skills that many people don't ever learn, so don't waste a single calorie beating yourself up about not having those skills. Once you start changing your behavior toward your under-confidence, and start being more socially active and comfortable, you will notice how many people do not have these skills. I know I didn't, and that's why I wrote this book. These exercises will soon become part of your natural behavior. Eventually you are going to say something unsolicited to every stranger you meet, just for the fun of it. You will have let go of who you were and are starting to discover who you can become.

Remember, when doing these exercises, manage your expectations. This is key to avoid traumatic setbacks. Don't get over-confident and aim for too much too soon. These exercises always hinge on Dosage, and the increase in Dosage is baby steps, not giant steps.

Don't forget that the real goal will be to connect with other people in a way that makes you realize we are all human, with social needs, who want to feel interesting, important, and appreciated. Beyond that, you want to be able to connect more deeply with those close to you so that you don't leave desires unspoken or curiosities unsatisfied, or love, appreciation, or gratitude unexpressed.

Finally, although this may seem to be mostly about meeting people, the same transformation that makes it possible for you to be comfortable with meeting anyone new is the same transformation that will help you take any bold action.

HOW TO FIND STRANGERS

I'm sure you're wondering how you are going to find all these strangers to talk to. I'll give you two ways: first, by realizing how often you actually run into people you don't know. You go to the supermarket, the drug store, your coffee place, your dry cleaners, and your job undoubtedly puts you in contact with people you don't know, unless you are on a submarine. Opportunities are everywhere.

The second way is by breaking out of your routine. Here's one of the big challenges for the unbold: you don't go anywhere new. By that I mean you have designed your life to encounter the same people over and over, and you don't move outside the safe circle of family and friends that you've established. This comfort circle is designed by you to protect you from new encounters where you feel awkward or under-confident. We need to break that protective wall in order to do these Boldness Exercises.

Go to a town meeting, or a class, or wander around the local mall. Sushi bars are natural environments to talk to the person next to you. Regular bars are often the same, but more of the people there have ulterior motives. Plus, alcohol has its drawbacks. Instead, sign up for an evening class in anything at all that interests you. Or join a club.

In short, get the heck out of your cave. Go out into all kinds of new places, whether they are shopping malls, restaurants, or coffee shops. There are five thousand Starbucks in the US alone, so you could start there. You don't need a justifiable reason to be in any of these public places. Later on, I'll have you going to places where you don't belong, just to show you that nothing bad happens. For now, choose places where anyone could go.

Basically, in order to talk to strangers, you need to encounter strangers. Maybe you're so shy that you don't know the names of the people you work with. This would be a great place to start. Once a day, meet someone in your place of business, and store their name in your memory, or even a notebook.

I now get the uncontrollable urge to talk to a complete stranger whenever I encounter one. Especially if I see them being uncomfortable, or not talking or making eye contact. Then I want to pierce through that and engage them. I still feel that tug of shyness some of the time, but it's like a little crack in the sidewalk rather than a ten-foot-high wall. I'm not powerless over my shyness anymore, and that's the greatest feeling. When it comes up, I acknowledge it as part of who I have been, but not who I am or will ever have to be. I'm superbold. I can summon it anytime I want. And I want you to get to the point where you have that same feeling, that urge to talk to everyone. If I can get there, you can too.

SAVOR THE VICTORIES

What we often forget to do in life is take the time to celebrate. What I want to make sure you do at the end of each day is stop and reflect on the Boldness Exercises that you did, and savor the moments, both the successes and "failures," because you ventured out of your comfort zone and that is something to be proud of.

Give yourself a little pat on the back. A little gold star on your calendar. A bite of chocolate or a mouthful of your favorite ice cream. Because each of these are genuine achievements and, more importantly, they are building blocks for the launchpad to your dreams.

So, take the time each day and savor the moments on your journey to superboldness. At the end of each week and each month, sit and review all that you've done. It will be cause to celebrate. You are on your way.

CHAPTER 14

EXERCISES: LEVEL 2 AND LEVEL 3

You've laid a basic foundation of outgoing behavior in Level 1, so now it's time to build on that confidence and broaden your skills. You've widened your comfort zone, and the Boldness Exercises in Level 1 should start to become your new standard social behavior. If you are not very low on the boldness scale, you may have breezed through some of the exercises in Level 1, or even skipped them. Either way, this is where the fun begins.

I remind you now that boldness is about summoning a bit of courage, in that it requires the willingness to be socially and even physically uncomfortable to achieve a certain result. In the case of the exercises, tapping into personal courage is about developing social skills and ease in social situations, until finally any type of bold action becomes possible for you.

This is why Level 2 Boldness Exercises are meant to push you, not just to say things, but to do things. Boldness isn't just about meeting people and achieving better social skills. It's about moving through the world in a completely different way, a more empowered state.

Level 2 Boldness Exercises don't have to be done in order, although I have built a progression in them. The idea is to pick one, do it that day, and then the next day pick another. You can repeat the exercises as often as you like, but your goal should be to do each one at least ten times before you move to Level 3. That is the minimum, but the true gauge of when you are ready for the next level is when you feel comfortable enough to do these Level 2 exercises without hesitation. Recognizing your plateau, as I said.

If you find yourself doing more than one a day, that's even better. Once a day is the minimum. There is no maximum!

You should know the PRIDE Method steps by now, so I'm not going to repeat them with every exercise. You are going to find yourself talking to service personnel in various businesses like restaurants, grocery stores, bars, and shopping malls, as well as random strangers everywhere. You'll be doing activities that will undoubtedly make you uncomfortable. (That's the point!)

As always, with each exercise, write in your journal what you discovered, how the exercise went, how you reacted, and what you might have done differently, or what you missed on the PRIDE steps.

And then celebrate the victories.

LEVEL 2 EXERCISES

1. **In a restaurant, learn your waiter or waitress's name.** When you're ready to leave, find them, shake their hand, and thank them, repeating their name as you do. (This is a great way of cultivating general friendliness.) You can also do this with a bartender. But don't cheat and get drunk first.

2. **Ask a stranger for an opinion about something you're wearing.** This means that you should be wearing something different or worth asking about. It can also be something goofy or inappropriate, which just adds to the fun, especially

if you see them staring at you already. This could be a hat, a scarf, a T-shirt, or shoes. Doesn't matter. You could even ask if two of the things you are wearing go together.

3. **In a grocery store, ask someone if they know the difference between two produce items.** For example, ask about a regular cucumber and Persian one, or a tangerine and a tangelo. Then don't buy either of them. (This is because a shy person ends up buying something they don't need or want, simply because they feel like they must because they asked about it. You are going to resist that urge.) If you're feeling under-confident at first, start with a grocery clerk, but eventually move on to your fellow shoppers. This can expand to almost anything in any store that you ask a stranger for an opinion about.

4. **For an entire day, ask everyone you meet their name.** Try to remember all of them. This is obviously a broader exercise than just doing it a few times a day, as in Level 1. The idea is that you are prevented from excluding anyone. You'll know when you finally get strong at Level 2, because you'll actually start remembering names instead of forgetting them the instant people tell you.

5. **Ask a waiter for something you don't need.** The more absurd, the better. Ask for a side of peanut butter in an Italian restaurant, or grass-fed butter for your vegetables. You'll notice that the exercises are starting to demand some creativity on your part. I want you to get more mentally nimble, which means you are both prepared and relaxed, and can improvise more. The more unbold you are (or were until you did Level 1), the more challenging this will be, because the old you wouldn't even ask for something extra that you wanted.

6. **Ask someone sitting near you in a restaurant what they are eating.** It might be more fun if it's really obvious what it is,

like a cheeseburger. They'll look at you like you're nuts, but they'll most likely answer. Then you can say, "Oh, I thought it might be a turkey burger." Conversation might ensue, or not, but you're just trying to engage a stranger. Don't forget to thank them. If you're feeling under-confident at the outset, start in a sushi bar. It'll be easy. That's what everyone does there. Then branch out.

7. **Be super positive with five people.** Say to the first five people you encounter in your day, "I don't know about you, but I'm having one of the best days of my life. I hope you are too." If you're feeling on a roll, do it all day.

8. **Introduce two people to each other at a party or event.** Offer effusive compliments about each of them, how wonderful and amazing they are, going into great detail, to the point of near embarrassment. And then walk away. You'll feel surprisingly good about it. And you know what they'll talk about after you're gone? How great you are. This may require you to meet some new people at the party first to gather your material. That ups the ante. Go for it.

9. **Go to a restaurant and eat alone.** And don't hide in your phone. At most, read a book, but ideally just sit there with a smile on your face the whole meal. Totally immerse yourself in the discomfort. Register how lonely and alone it makes you feel. I guarantee that you won't always feel that way. You'll be imagining that a bunch of strangers are looking at you and thinking, "Look at that sad, lonely person eating alone." *And you'll actually care what these strangers think!* I want you to bathe in the irrelevance and absurdity of your reaction.

10. **Smile at every single person you meet for an entire day.** If they smile back, say hi. Ideally, this includes plenty of strangers. You will experience the full range of reactions. Relax and

enjoy the variety of them. Marvel at how differently people respond to a stranger smiling at them.

11. **For an entire day, make eye contact with everyone you interact with.** Keep track of how often you don't, and you look away. (You might need to give yourself a break at some point, but we're looking for at least 90 percent here.) Observe the variety of reactions to eye contact. Calculate where that person might fall on the boldness scale.

12. **Talk to a stranger while riding in an elevator.** Make a random observation or ask what they do on their floor. Or say something positive, like, "I know not everyone thinks this, but I love Mondays." Elevators are a classic environment where people don't talk. But you will discover that they don't mind at all. They think it's as weird as you do that no one talks. If there are no elevators where you work, go use one in a nearby hotel. (By the way, if you're in Australia this doesn't count, because everyone talks to you in elevators there.)

13. **Buy something you don't need and then return it.** (Make sure they have a 100 percent return policy!) Return it with a big smile on your face and try to give as little explanation as possible as to why you don't want it. Unbold people hate to do this even when they decide they don't want something. This exercise will show you that all this stuff you're playing in your head just isn't true. Most employees could care less if you bring something back. And most stores are fine with it. Even if they aren't, and they don't take it back, the exercise worked.

14. **Bring something back to a store that you've used or worn and try to return it.** (This is an expansion of the previous exercise.) If you're really bold, try it without the receipt. The bolder you are, the more used the item should look. The goal is to have your request be so ridiculous that you're sure it

will be refused. If they tell you their return policy is no returns, then act all disappointed. Taking it to an even higher level, bring the used item back after the return date limit. Or entirely used, like a pair of shoes. (Zappos doesn't count. They'll take anything back within a year, the first time. Besides, I'm talking about someplace where you actually have to walk inside.)

15. **Go to a bar, and don't leave until you interact with someone.** Have at least a brief conversation, including learning their name. It could be with someone your gender or the opposite. If you're gay, this doesn't count as an exercise if you go into a gay bar. It's too easy to strike up a conversation in a gay bar. If you don't drink alcohol, do this in a coffee shop. Or just order soda water in the bar. A professional bartender won't bat an eye.

16. **In a department store, ask another shopper to help you choose a tie, or a shirt, or a blouse, or an accessory.** A few people will likely decline to help. If you start with, "You look very well dressed. Could you suggest..." then you are employing the embedded compliment. That always helps.

17. **When staying in a hotel, call and ask for all sorts of crazy stuff.** A robe, slippers, hangers, free ice cream, even. Ask if someone will come to your room and iron something for you. Your ultimate goal is an "Uh, no, we can't do that." You will find that you will get many more things than you expected.

18. **Walk backward into a movie theater without showing your ticket.** At least half the time no one will stop you and try or ask to punch your ticket. Do buy a ticket, though. This is not scam training.

19. **Introduce yourself to a complete and total stranger.** But first, go to an area of town where you've never been to

before. This gives you "diplomatic immunity." Most likely this will happen on the sidewalk. You're not going to know anyone, so you can be foolish and not worry about it. And I would like you to be a little bit foolish. Say, "I'm new to the area. Do they have any interesting Asian food here?" Or any one of a million questions you can ask. Try to go three sentences, and get their name if you can. See how much information they want to give you. Keep asking questions. Then thank them and walk away.

20. **Ask a stranger if they have change for a twenty.** This will arouse suspicion in most people. Which is the point of the exercise. I want you to get comfortable with accepting suspicion, even though you are innocent. It's harmless, unless you turn it into harm. They are having a normal reaction to a stranger expecting them to be trusting. In fact, if anyone gives you change, I'll be shocked. Either way, the exercise worked.

21. **Pretend to be choking in a public place.** See if someone steps up to perform the Heimlich maneuver on you. I'm kidding! Don't do this! It's a terrible way to meet people!

There is a lot to do here, and you could feel really uncomfortable trying most of these exercises, but you will have dozens of little breakthroughs, and you will be steadily reprogramming yourself.

A win for you will be when you have that feeling that you went outside your comfort zone, met someone new, and had a real exchange. It may not have been deep and meaningful, but for at least a moment or two it was a connection. Maybe, if you did it right, they felt better about themselves after encountering you. That's when you really start to appreciate the satisfaction that can only come from that experience. I hope to get you addicted to it.

THE CONSPIRATORIAL EXCHANGE

You may find yourself in a situation where you can talk to one person about a third person who is visible but not part of the conversation. This is what I call the conspiratorial exchange, where you don't necessarily say something negative or critical, but make an observation about that third person that you share as a first line with a stranger. It's usable at parties, in elevators, in food lines, anywhere that you can both see the third person, but they cannot hear you.

For example, I was just in the elevator with two people, a man and a woman. The man got out at a lower floor than the woman, and I turned to her and said, "That was a serious amount of cologne to be wearing." The woman looked at me and said, "Right? So, I'm not crazy. That was a lot." And I said, "I imagine sitting next to him all day at work is pretty intense."

She laughed, then got out at her floor.

It was a harmless critique of someone. That's the key. Or it could be that you observe someone wearing something very bold—a purple hat or bright pink shirt—and you could say, "I couldn't wear that, but they pull it off." Make it positive, not critical, so that it invites the conspiratorial response and also encourages the other person to not have a negative judgment.

This can be deployed whenever you are doing one of your "talk to a stranger" Boldness Exercises. Or just for the fun of it.

LEVEL 3 EXERCISES

Now I'm hoping—and expecting—that you're ready to really challenge yourself. At this next level, you are deliberately going to seek out the embarrassment you once feared.

One of the goals of the Level 3 exercises will be for you to do things where you expect to be asked or told to leave someplace or stop doing something. You'll be amazed at how hard this is, relative to your beliefs or expectations.

Remember you are making a game of this, striving for failure, with the lesson being how wrong you are about what will happen. As you get bolder, you will realize that you can press the issue and manage to get away with even more. No one will be harmed in these Boldness Exercises, and no laws will be broken. But you will break free of many of your preconceived notions about barriers, limitations, and obstacles.

Some of the exercises will seem a bit absurd or pointless. Don't judge; just do them. You're not trying to achieve anything except strengthening your boldness muscle for when you need it.

Think of it just like physical exercises. If you think about it, there really isn't any point to doing bench presses either. You're not likely to need to get an extremely heavy weight off your chest anytime in your life. But it makes you stronger. These exercises will do the same and come in handy when you do need to get something off your chest. (Now that was just brilliant, wasn't it?)

Essentially, the Level 3 exercises are designed specifically to make you extremely uncomfortable. Until you aren't.

As you do each exercise, continue to follow the steps of the PRIDE Method, and then make notes in your journal on what happened. One of these a day will probably be plenty at first, especially since you should be incorporating other Boldness Exercises from Level 1 and 2 into your daily behavior. At this stage, I hope that many of them stop being exercises and are part of your normal behavior. Of course, do more as you feel more comfortable.

1. **Put earbuds in and sing out loud in a public place.** You'll know it's working when people give you strange looks. You will not die. Do it for as long as you can stand it, then leave the area. Each day, make sure you extend the amount of time you do it.

2. **Call a customer service line.** Try to return something that is over a year old, or try to get them to fix a product that is not their brand.

3. **Wear a Band-Aid on your face.** Do it for as long as you can stand it. Revel in the heightened feeling of self-consciousness, knowing that at any time you can take the Band-Aid off. The next time you do it, make it an even more awkward place that you put it. Right across your nose, or your lip. The goal is to eventually do it for an entire day. People will stare at you and ask you what happened. Enjoy making something up.

4. **Use the restroom opposite of your gender.** You know what happens? Nothing. At most, someone will look at you oddly. And don't, when you come out, under any circumstances, resort to giving any excuse as to why you did it. Just smile at anyone who looks at you harshly. It is not a crime. (And if you're a male, put the seat back down!)

5. **Wear something you** never **would normally wear.** It could be an outlandish shirt or blouse, or wild shoes, or a hat. It just has to be something you feel very uncomfortable wearing in public. Used clothing stores are great for these types of things, especially on the funkier side of town. Wear it at least four hours. Embrace the discomfort. Enjoy the feedback.

6. **Wear a wig in public.** A good one. For at least four hours. If you're a woman this might be easier, so it has to be a radically different hairstyle than yours (and looks worse, ideally). For a man, you're going for almost a toupee look. But either way, it has to be radically different than how you normally wear your hair, in length, color, and style. Then, with it on, go and do a Level 1 or 2 exercise. Enjoy the fact that you are essentially in disguise and get out and talk to people. You're incognito. Guys could even try a fake mustache as well. You'll be surprised how it will embolden you, as if you are someone else. Take the lesson to heart.

7. **Ask someone to scratch your back.** (This one is for guys only.) Ask a stranger, in a public place. Expect, of course, to be

refused—this is one exercise where you will rarely get cooperation. Give an explanation of why you can't reach the spot—your arms are stiff from exercise, your nails are too short to be effective, whatever.

8. **Walk into the back room of a grocery store.** There will be alarms going off in your head saying, "I shouldn't be back here," but there will be no other alarms going off. It's not a bank vault. In fact, it is not a crime to go into the back room. Most likely someone will say something to you like, "Can I help you?" or "Are you lost?" They may say, "You can't come back here," and then you can apologize and leave. But nothing bad will happen! No one will beat you over the head with a hammer, nor will you be charged with trespassing.

9. **Sit in a fast food restaurant with takeout food from somewhere else.** Just sit at one of the tables and start eating. Maybe even use the napkins and utensils, if you are feeling extra bold. At most, someone will come up to you and either stop you and ask you to leave, or they will be so much in shock that they will ask if they can bring you something to drink. Refuse. Produce your own beverage. Maybe ask for a cup with ice. Most likely, nothing will happen at all. Warning: don't do this in a place that is so crowded that you are preventing their paying customers from sitting. We are not striving to be inconsiderate, ever. Also, leave a tip.

10. **Ask a stranger if you can use their napkin.** Obviously, this is in a restaurant. Alternatively, it could be their towel at the beach. I actually did this once because I had forgotten my towel and I could see that this couple had a spare towel and were going swimming. I almost didn't ask, but I made it an exercise. And then it turned out I knew them. That's what can happen when you're bold and have become fearless of the harmless.

11. **Challenge a stranger to a game you've never played before.** Like chess or gin rummy. If they agree, ask if they could teach you how to play. Or ask someone to play a game with you, probably a card game, and offer to teach them. Expect to be refused or brushed off. (As if I have to keep saying that. But I feel compelled to remind you.)

12. **Come up with your own challenge.** Get creative as you get bolder. Find signs prohibiting you from doing something, like a retail store that insists that you don't bring sale items into the restroom. And then do it. See if anyone says anything. This has a dual purpose, as do most of the exercises. You will find out that most of the time, nothing will happen.

I'm not saying shoplift here. Do not commit any crimes as part of your exercises. But you will see signs everywhere prohibiting things, sometimes for silly reasons. The point is to countermand your inner voice that is saying, "Don't do it. You'll get caught. It will be embarrassing to be told you can't do it." You are *trying* to be told that you can't do it, precisely so that you can experience how little impact it will have. What will also be happening is you'll be building up your rejection callus, and you won't really care if someone stops you.

When you start to invent your own Boldness Exercises, think about this: do you know how much security guards make? It's not a lot. It's usually not enough to go to any trouble at all to prevent anything from happening or to reprimand someone or detain them. They actually don't have a right to detain you. They are essentially mannequins with security badges, scarecrows to keep people from doing things. But no matter what, they are unlikely to make a big deal out of anything. (And if they do, you still win the exercise.)

If a sign says, "Employees Only," look at that as your invitation. The lesson here is simple: nothing bad will happen to you! You will not be arrested or physically attacked. You will be told by someone that you can't be doing what you're doing. You'll also be amazed at how reluctant people are to say that. (Except for the rare few who absolutely revel in it. You know the type.)

You are going for that as the result, and if you don't get it, then your venture doesn't count, and you have to find another place to harmlessly invade until someone kicks you out. It could take you all day. You will figure out that the only thing keeping you out are the signs themselves. Zero other enforcement.

When doing this exercise myself, I've been told, "This is for employees only!" And I say, "Oh, I am an employee. Just not here." And then I leave, after I let that sink in. They think I'm an idiot.

As you do this, you will have hesitation, maybe even paralysis, but the fact that you are *trying deliberately* to be told to get out will make it easy and perhaps even fun. And you will be doing no harm to anyone. Of course, don't go into a sterile room or a truly secure military area or something like that. That's not what we're going for here.

You are going to deliberately put yourself in a situation where someone is going to either tell you to leave or makes you leave. That's the game, and you have to treat it that way. That is the winning failure. You want wet armpits, stuttering, clammy hands, scared eyes. You're actually going for that instead of shying away from it (literally). You will find this so liberating, you'll be like an acrophobic who just bungee-jumped for the first time, and can't wait to do it again.

You have dozens, if not hundreds, of places you tell yourself you ought not go into. This transfers directly to the same kind of story you tell yourself about encounters with people. You may get rejected. You may not get the sale. You may get turned away. But nothing truly bad will actually happen. You will be no worse off than if you didn't do the thing at all.

Come up with some of these and go out and do them. But keep doing all the Boldness Exercises until you start to feel strong enough that they don't even seem like a real challenge. That could take some time, on average eight to ten weeks, but this is the period where you will advance in boldness in a significant way. Then you'll be ready for Level 4.

CHAPTER 15

EXERCISES: LEVEL 4 AND LEVEL 5

LEVEL 4 EXERCISES

T**he Level 4 Boldness Exercises are a combination of real-life situations** and some wild activities designed solely to build your boldness muscle.

All the standard PRIDE Method steps apply, but be even more introspective in your journal entries, reflecting on what's changed about you, how you see people differently, and how they react to you differently. And really savor both the failures and successes.

You'll notice there are a lot more Boldness Exercises at this level. That's because some of them you may only do once or twice. Some of them may take several tries before you get up the nerve to complete them. Also, they are in no particular order because some of them you can only do when a situation presents itself.

Exercise 1

Single out the shiest person in the room. This could be at a party or any social or business event. At first, just watch the person's behavior. Study them and see yourself in them, or some part of your former self, like the defense mechanisms as they stand by themselves, running a dozen judgments a minute through their head as they scan the room. How long ago was that you?

Now, introduce yourself to them, walking right up, engaging them and, after a reasonable conversation, break away. Part two is to then find another group and introduce yourself, and eventually invite that shy person into it. Think of it as throwing a lifeline to that person who once was you.

Exercise 2

Ask some people on the beach if you can leave your stuff on their blanket while you jump in the water. They will likely say no. That's the point. We are now pushing the boundaries of when someone would reasonably go along with your request, and yet you will find that some people will. (Be sure not to leave anything valuable!) You will feel the boldness muscle developing when it happens. There are alternatives to this, especially if you're not near the water, like if you have a child, asking if someone will watch your kid while you order at a fast-food restaurant. You will get some seriously disturbed looks, and possibly some admonishment from a concerned parent. If someone by chance agrees, don't actually leave your child with them. Oh, and don't ask someone to watch your bag at the airport. Duh.

Exercise 3

Put on headphones and sing and dance in public to what you're listening to. If you don't trust your voice is good, even better. This expands on the Level 3 Boldness Exercise, adding the dancing, which takes way more self-confidence. It can be anywhere: grocery store, bus stop, a shopping mall, or right out on the sidewalk. The more uncomfortable you imagine yourself feeling in a place, the more it becomes something to work your way up to. That's the Dosage control here.

Once you've done this in a fairly innocuous environment, it's time to push the envelope. Find a more crowded place, a more unexpected place, like on a bus or in an airport. The goal is to get some really strange looks, a few people laughing, and maybe one or two people encouraging you. I think you'll be shocked at how many more people are delighted than weirded out. Some of them might even be a little envious. When they stare, smile back.

Exercise 4

Ask if you can borrow someone's cell phone. You're looking for a no here, to find out that you don't die. Your Preparation is to make up a fairly lame reason why you need to borrow it.

Exercise 5

Walk into a chocolate shop and yell, "I love chocolate!" I guarantee you that some people will smile, and no one will throw you in jail or a mental hospital. You can repeat this exercise, replacing the chocolate shop for any other store you might be passionate about (or not!): an ice cream shop, an antique store, or Costco.

Exercise 6

Be so loud that people are compelled to tell you to be quiet. Do it in a restaurant or a movie theater before it starts, or on an airplane. If you have a fear of being shushed or an angry reaction to it (like I do), even better. Get over it. Nothing happens. You will never die from being shushed. They will forget about it the moment you give them a lame excuse, like you have water in your ear or you're losing your hearing and haven't adjusted to your new hearing aid, and you apologize. Try it, because you need to find out that no injury will come to you, and you can even be polite about being rude. Do it with a smile. You'll also be surprised at how loud you have to get before someone says something. Why? Because they're too shy to speak up!

Exercise 7

Walk into a coffee shop and say, "Can I have everyone's attention? I lost my car keys. Did anyone find them in the parking lot?" The whole public address thing is a huge challenge, but this gives you an excuse. Of course, you're making up the reason, but it's still a very reasonable thing to do.

Exercise 8

Sit in a handicapped seat at an airport or bus station, but only if there are several empty ones. Obviously get up if someone handicapped needs the seat. You're not hurting anyone. You're just afraid of the "rules." There is no penalty for sitting there. You won't get a ticket. It's not like you're parking in a handicapped spot. Don't *ever* do that, by the way.

Exercise 9

Bring a pork roast to a bar mitzvah. No, don't. That's a joke. There's bold and there's ignorant. Don't cross that line or even go near it. These exercises are never about being rude or inconsiderate. Loud, maybe, but that's it.

Exercise 10

Do an open mic night at a comedy club. Three minutes. Don't worry about being funny. Many other people won't be that night.

Exercise 11

Hand out comedy club tickets in a public place. This is likely the comedy club where you did the open mic. They are always putting people on busy street corners to hand out free tickets. These are comedians who are desperate for stage time, and the deal they make with the club is to accost strangers and try to get them to come to the comedy club. It's a tough gig, and it will make you tough. You can replace this with volunteering to get people to sign a petition for a cause you support. Massive rejection will come your way. And you won't die.

Exercise 12

Panhandle for an hour. That will be plenty of time to give you an idea what real rejection feels like.

Exercise 13

If you're single, try online dating. But here's the requirement: deliberately aim for someone who is interesting rather than attractive. This is the big trap for shy people, that we use appearance as our excuse for not meeting someone. We set our standard so high that naturally everyone is excluded except the people who we have the lowest percentage chance with.

Here is the strange truth people who've been married or dated very attractive people know that most others don't: you get used to their beauty. In fact, if their personality is unattractive, they become unattractive to you. I've seen super-studs turn a woman off in three sentences. And I've seen women who people would call a ten turn into a three to the person who is constantly waiting for her to get ready to go out.

Exercise 14

When you find yourself in a situation that disturbs or upsets or irritates you, summon the opposite reaction to it, then speak. First, change what it means to you, as I laid out in Chapter 11. Then find a way to say something friendly, even complimentary, to that person even if it doesn't relate to what's bothering you. But if it does relate, all the better. This goes beyond what I had you do in Chapter 11, because now you are going outside of your head and expressing yourself and saying the reverse of what your original reaction was.

If, for example, you find yourself in an elevator with someone wearing such an overwhelming amount of perfume that you're almost gagging, say, "That's a lovely scent you've chosen." (And leave out the part about how they put on too much of it.) Or someone may be talking too loudly on their phone in a public place, and you get to say, "Isn't it nice to always be able to stay in touch with people?" (Who knows? They could just be doing a Level 4 Boldness Exercise!)

Exercise 15

Sing karaoke and really put your body into it. Imitate Jagger or Beyoncé. Don't just stand there. And hey, don't forget: you don't need to know how to sing. There are lots of easy choices. Rap music is technically just reciting rhymes, mostly about women's body parts and guns. And Eminem "sings" almost completely in monotone. You will eventually need one or two of your own personal karaoke songs that you can bust out whenever you're asked to go to a place. This is called Preparation.

Exercise 16

Ask someone in a restaurant if you can try the dish they're eating. You'll be amazed at how many people will let you. Start off by just asking how they like it and proceed from there.

I once walked up to two women in a restaurant and asked them how the Mexican corn was. They ended up offering me a piece. This is how adept I've become at approaching strangers. Will it work all the time? No. Will people snub me, ignore me, or even rudely dismiss me? Yes. Sometimes. Their loss. Not mine. The corn was excellent, by the way.

Exercise 17

Memorize a toast. Or a few of them—a funny one, a serious one, and an inspiring one. Be the one who steps up and gives one. When you are in a large group, a dinner or whatever, stand up, tap a glass with a knife until you have everyone's attention, and then offer your toast, ideally to the host, or to express your appreciation for being part of the group. Eventually you need to do this without having memorized a toast, and just offer your thoughts extemporaneously.

Exercise 18

Go into a bar alone and buy someone a drink. Not as a pickup move. Say you're celebrating waking up this morning, or something equally innocuous. If you've got the cash, buy two people a drink at the same time. You could even say to the bartender, "I'd like to buy the two nicest people at the bar a drink. You decide." Or say to the people around you in a bar, "I will buy anyone a drink who can tell me a joke I haven't heard." The way you will decide the winner is if you can say the punchline yourself or not. And you've added a public address challenge to the exercise.

Exercise 19

Ask a stranger for a hug. Low percentage results on this one, to be sure, but you may be surprised who steps up and gives you a squeeze.

Exercise 20

Dress up when people are dressed down. Wear a tie, or a suit, or a fabulous dress. Cross-dressing is allowed for either gender. I'm not kidding. Once you've cross-dressed, then you'll be amazed how hard it will be to feel embarrassed by anything you do.

Exercise 21

In a restaurant or coffee shop, ask someone if they will swap tables with you. Make up a reason, or don't even give one.

Exercise 22

Go to an acting audition. You will undoubtedly be terrible, and even if you're not, rejection is 99 percent of the typical actor's experience. It will have to be a nonunion audition, or you won't be allowed in. But hey, that might turn out to be the entire challenge. Show up at an audition you know they won't let you in for.

Exercise 23

Play a musical instrument for tips in front of a store or in a city square. Badly, ideally. Get someone to pay you to stop. (If you actually do this, I will be so impressed with you. I've never even done this exercise myself!)

LEVEL 5 EXERCISES

At Level 5, you are the creator of the Boldness Exercises. You will need to be totally honest and introspective and determine what it is that you're still afraid of. Then come up with Boldness Exercises that gradually help you work your way up to feeling comfortable in those situations.

Level 5 is endless because you are going to work at becoming bolder for the rest of your life. Because now it's fun, satisfying, and rewarding. This is how you become superbold, creating situations and summoning boldness in each of them.

Some things to keep in mind:

- Control the Dosage, but increase it on your own.
- Aim for failure as part of the design.
- Don't worry about making people uncomfortable.
- Don't harm anyone in any way, or scam anyone.
- Get suggestions from your wing person if you can't think of anything.
- Do something every day (of course!).

Eventually, you are going to look at all sorts of situations that require boldness, and you'll approach them just like one of these Boldness Exercises. Your comfort zone will get larger and larger, and your dreams closer and closer.

BOLD AND HUMBLE

While many people consider bold people to be cocky and full of themselves, in my experience, the people who live bold lives also come from a place of great humility. I have had the opportunity to meet some very successful people over the years, and I can assure you that 95 percent of them are humble and grateful for the opportunities and success they've enjoyed.

A perfect example is Sir Richard Branson, who built the Virgin empire and made himself a multibillionaire. I've never met a man more humble and down-to-earth than he is. I had the good fortune to be taking a course on Necker Island, his resort in the British Virgin Islands. While playing tennis there, I ruptured my Achilles tendon. When he heard about it, he sought me out and asked if I wanted to play chess. We played and also had several personal conversations over the next few days, and my high admiration for him was cemented. He has a generous heart, a playful spirit, and values his family above all else.

The late Tony Hsieh, the powerhouse CEO who turned Zappos into a billion-dollar company in ten years, was just the same. When I took a tour of his facility, he met me and took me to lunch. As we sat down to eat, the first words out of his mouth were, "So, how can I help you?" Remember, he didn't know me at all.

I asked him if my whole team could come and take a tour to learn from the inspiring work culture he had created, and he said, "Of course." I ran into him again a year later at the South by Southwest Conference in Austin, and we sat in a cocktail lounge where he performed card tricks for my wife.

Both these men had absolutely nothing to gain from me. They dwarfed my meager success a thousand times over. And yet, I count them among the most decent, humble, compassionate businesspeople I've known. As well as the boldest. Bold people make enough mistakes—often huge ones—that it keeps them fairly humble. It just doesn't stop them.

So, don't believe that self-defeating voice that tells you that being bold makes you an arrogant jerk. Those successful people who are jerks were always that way, long before they made it. Bold people are almost always humble, and I expect you will be too, no matter how bold you become.

CHAPTER 16

WHAT NOT TO DO

As you move along the path to your ultimate boldness, I'd like to help you avoid some of the classic behavioral mistakes that you might make along the way. Consider this next section guiding principles on What Not to Do.

Most of these principles you can start incorporating immediately into your life, as they are not Boldness Exercises, but rules for better social interaction. Some will be "Aha" moments for you, and easy to change, while others may take a while to unlearn. Knowing the principles is half the battle because then you are on the path to self-awareness, and you'll catch yourself doing the behaviors.

If you find you violated one of these "Don't Do" principles when doing the Boldness Exercises, make a note in your journal, especially if they caused a specific reaction in the encounter. That will solidify the observation and help you eliminate the behavior going forward.

DON'T MONOLOGUE

Monologuing—talking in an unbroken stream for a minute or two or five—is deadly to first encounters.

Monologuing is often driven by anxiety. And it's very easy to lapse into stream-of-consciousness high-speed babbling when you get in new social situations. Learn to sense when your mouth is running out of control. Stop. Take a breath. You MUST hand over the mic, so to speak. If you realize you've been monologuing, you can always say something lightly apologetic, like, "But enough about me..." and ask them almost anything about themselves.

Another option you could say is "Sorry, I get excited about this sort of thing. How's your day going?"

Or, "Forgive me, I tend to babble when I meet someone interesting."

(Notice the embedded compliment? Magic.)

Also, monologuing is the opposite of Power Tool #6, Using Suspense. There's definitely no suspense when you're giving excessive detail without a pause. Which makes monologuing the opposite of a Power Tool. You can usually see it in the person's eyes. They start to look away and maybe even yawn.

You want to defeat this tendency because it could derail an opportunity very easily. Imagine, for example, that you've finally decided to speak up in a business meeting, and you have the group's attention. You launch into cocaine-speak, verbal diarrhea, and suddenly everyone's eyes glaze over. Total fail. You want to be able to inject your powerful thoughts and observations calmly, in control, saying what you want to and how much you want to, and weighing the option to speak or not. So be on the alert for monologuing and slam on the brakes.

Remember, if you're talking more than you're listening, you're not interesting.

DON'T PLAY "TOP THIS!"

Let's say you've climbed Mount Everest. Is this an amazing achievement? Of course it is. But to bring it up early in a conversation, especially where the topic isn't mountain climbing, sounds like you can't wait to impress people with what you've done. Since not many people have summited Everest, it's pretty hard to top someone when they say they climbed the highest mountain in the world and didn't die. So where exactly does that conversation go from there?

This applies to bringing up your achievements even on a much smaller scale. Here's a key lesson in meeting people: launching into a statement that sounds like you're playing "Top This" will bring most conversations to a screeching halt. Because that's not really what attracts people. They love movie stars and rock stars, and occasionally a successful businessperson or adventurer, but they don't want everyone they meet to have some sort of high-level achievement that they can't possibly rival in the conversation.

I'm not against adventure. I love it and I'm a bit of an adrenaline junkie myself. But I learned not to roll it out for the bragging rights, because it's a conversation stopper. Or it turns into a contest about who has done the most amazing thing. There's no room to reveal vulnerability, or express human interest or anything resembling a basis for a real relationship. It's attempting to impress, to one-up the other person.

So, if someone tells you they just got back from Rome, don't immediately reply with, "Oh, yeah, I was there in 2005, saw U2 play a concert in the Colosseum, blah, blah, blah, (Top that!)." Instead, say, "Really? What was your favorite moment?" Think about those two responses. Who do you think someone would rather continue talking to?

Stop trying to be more interesting and be more interested in the other person.

The same goes for being funny. This can quickly turn into a "Top this line" contest, with each person striving to come up with some witty, clever, or comedic response. Enter at your own risk. One-upmanship always peters out eventually, because by its very nature, there is a winner and a loser.

That's not where I want to take you with boldness. I want you to achieve real, lasting dreams. Sure, go ahead and climb a mountain, or do an Ironman challenge, or learn sword-swallowing. Do it for the fun of it or to challenge yourself physically and mentally. Don't do it to be interesting. Your bold pursuit of your dreams will make you interesting—even more so when you are modest about those achievements, and more interested in the other person's dreams and how far along they are on their path.

Here's a trick to stop yourself: when you are about to tell someone the achievement you consider relevant and intriguing, instead ask them about something they may have done that is similar. For example, when they say they love tennis, don't tell them you went to Wimbledon last year; instead, say, "What's the most amazing match you've seen?" And listen. And then *never* tell them you went to Wimbledon. Believe me, it won't be easy—you'll be dying to bring it up. But it will work like magic because you shut down the "Top this!" urge.

In short, conversation is not a competition. Ironically, you win it by letting the other person top you. Let them get the biggest laugh or tell the best story. Being charismatic isn't winning everyone's attention. It's making everyone feel better about themselves.

DON'T BE A KNOW-IT-ALL

Using your big IQ and vast knowledge as a way to be interesting is a recipe for loneliness. You are more likely to find yourself alienating people because you are so desperate to be someone who knows more than anyone else. I know you're afraid of the embarrassment of being wrong. But have you ever noticed people gravitating toward a know-it-all? Someone with all the answers, with all the facts that contradict what someone else just said? I'll bet you haven't, because they are masters at repelling people. I know, because sometimes I've been that person. Worked like a curse, not a charm.

But I learned. Now I don't correct people. I even let them tell me what I already know, rather than saying that I already know it. I don't interrupt with, "Yes, I do that already, or I learned that years ago," or some conversation torpedo like that. Because it doesn't endear you to anyone, and it doesn't impress anyone. It just makes you feel a little better about yourself.

The same is true for giving advice. If you feel compelled to give advice about something, ask if the person is interested in hearing it. Which does not sound like, "Hey, you know what I would do in that situation?" There's no option for them to refuse, so you get to school them. How nice for them. Instead, say, "Some other time, if you're interested, I'll tell you what I did in a similar situation." Now they have the option of asking to hear it now, or keep talking, which is the real goal. (Even though giving advice can be so satisfying!)

Also, don't correct people's grammar. Believe me, I know how tempting it is when someone says, "Just between you and I," and you so desperately want to say, "You mean, between you and *me*, don't you?" Let it go. Lousy schools and texting have destroyed proper grammatical usage, and you're not going to fix it. It really doesn't matter, except to make you feel smart.

Don't have all the answers. Let someone else have them. Add something interesting and relevant, but not by contradicting them. Sure, it's fun to get in a deep conversation about global warming, but if you are on opposite poles (get it?), you're not going to change the other person's mind, nor will they convince you. Talk about movies instead. Or even better, try to understand their point of view and how it was formed. You just might learn something.

Catch yourself whenever you find yourself having all the answers or correcting people. Slam on the brakes and change direction.

You'll notice that there are no Boldness Exercises involving you sharing your vast knowledge or making an observation that makes you seem like the smartest person in the room. Why? Because the prime directive, the goal of each encounter, is to make that person feel better about themselves after interacting with you. Have you ever enjoyed being corrected by a stranger? Did it warm your heart and endear that person to you? I doubt it. Good friends can do this. But early on with people, it fails spectacularly.

Sarcasm is another way of making yourself feel smarter, but it doesn't make the person you are sarcastic with feel good. It may amuse others around you, but you're not making a friend. If they already are your friend, maybe they'll laugh along. And maybe not.

Now, if someone asks you the capital of North Dakota, then go for it if you know the answer. But you've been invited to share knowledge. That's a whole different thing. Now you can add to the conversation. But might it not be more interesting to see if you can tease the answer out of their own memory? Saying, "Wait, I know this. It's a guy's name. Something French," and then they jump in with "Pierre!" See the difference? You made them feel smart, instead of just blurting out the answer like you're watching *Jeopardy*. That's the art of conversation. (And I know that the response has to be in the form of a question on *Jeopardy*. Don't correct me.)

Your next argument with me may be to say, "So I don't get to have an opinion?" Sure you do. Just don't express it like it's a fact, like most people do with their opinions. Soften it, modify it, qualify it, and it becomes more palatable.

You could say, "Global warming is an absolute fact." Not a lot of wiggle room in that opinion. Or you could say, "I'm no expert, but from everything I've read, I've become convinced that global warming is real. But how do you see it?" And then, without judgment, pursue the formation of their opinion. You may decide you don't particularly like the person's viewpoint, or even the person, which means you don't need to put a lot of energy into changing (unsuccessfully) the mind of a complete stranger.

I disagree with the beliefs of many of my friends. But I'm so open-minded about it, sometimes they don't even realize I disagree with them. Or we can laugh about our disagreements and still love each other. I have a sneaking suspicion that I might not be right about everything. It's tempered my opinions and my judgments. You might try it.

DON'T DEAD-END THE DIALOGUE

Don't say things that bring the conversation to a halt. A lot of times, we have an initial encounter and say something that leads nowhere. It doesn't invite a meaningful response. It could be trying to be clever or cool, or doesn't show real interest in the person, or is negative in its perspective, or just plain weird. As I mentioned previously, it's easy to lapse into weird if you have no social training. Things like this often bring the conversation to an abrupt halt.

I was at an event recently, and I was talking to a friend of mine, who is a big, long-haired Texan, when this middle-aged man bounced up to us, looked at my friend, and said, "Hey, you remind me of Meatloaf!" First of all, that could have easily been taken as an insult, especially if you were unfamiliar with the '70s rock singer Meatloaf. But there was nowhere to go from that point for any of us. My friend just sort of nodded, and I eventually restarted the conversation by introducing myself to the invader. It was a classic example of saying something that leaves the other person at a loss as to how to respond. At the very least it's awkward and at the worst, it's cringeworthy.

And it's all because he was trying to be original. This is the mistake. I'll say it again: you don't need to be original in the first three sentences. It puts a lot of pressure on the other person to match it or even comprehend it. People aren't expecting glib or clever remarks to come at them out of nowhere, and you don't really know what's on their mind at the moment, so why tax their processor? Keep it simple and comprehensible.

There are also other ways to dead-end the conversation. One is by making a definitive statement of your opinion and doing it in a way that says you will brook no contradiction, saying something like, "In my experience, that's not true at all."

The other is to fizzle out the conversation with something like, "Well, that's life" or "Not much more to say about that." In both cases, the other person has to restart the conversation because you've stopped exchanging and eliciting responses. They might just say, "Well, nice to meet you," and walk away.

Always add to the conversation by saying, "Yes, and..." and asking questions. Don't ever make it the other's person's job to jump-start the stalled exchange.

Here are some more unproductive first things to say:

"What's up?" FAIL. This does not count as conversation or icebreaking or much of anything except a way to acknowledge someone you already know or are walking by without stopping.

The same goes for the casual "How you doin'?" or "How are ya?" and several things that are really just a hello that require the flimsiest of replies. You've done this many times, I'm sure. Has the conversation proceeded very far from there? Not often, I suspect. And I can almost guarantee it wasn't memorable for the other person. These are essentially friendly greetings and require more to turn the exchange into something meaningful.

If you did dead-end the conversation, then fix it. Ask a meaningful question and show interest. Feel free to apologize for being so absolute in your opinion, or weird, or incomprehensible. People will appreciate your self-awareness.

DON'T TRY TO BE FUNNY

I've mentioned this earlier, but I want to get more specific about attempting humor early on in an exchange.

"What?" you say. "People think I'm hilarious."

That may be true within your comfort circle. I'm just recommending you proceed with caution when you try to be funny with strangers.

The key word here is "try." Humor is risky business. Nervous people seldom pull it off. What's more, if you try to make a joke and no one laughs, you could end up making yourself more nervous. Use humor sparingly at the beginning of your venture into confidence, especially in the first few exchanges in a new encounter. And, for God's sake, don't memorize jokes to roll out at the first opportunity.

Also, be careful not to laugh at your own jokes or comments, particularly before other people do. You are laughing as a nervous reflex, rather than being funny. Here's a clue: when you are truly funny, other people laugh besides you.

Sometimes, if you find that you are laughing and other people aren't, it isn't that you aren't funny. It's just that you are adding a laugh track before they are ready, or your nervousness makes them too uncomfortable to laugh. If you've ever gone to a stand-up club on open mic night and seen an aspiring comedian who is extremely nervous onstage, you know what I mean. Even if they have good material, people aren't laughing because the comedian is still uncomfortable onstage.

So, relax, and don't try to be funny right away. Give them time to appreciate you before they have to appreciate your sense of humor. If you are attempting humor at some point in the conversation, just smile and wait to see if they get the joke. If you pause and they don't laugh, then you weren't that funny at that moment. It doesn't mean you aren't capable of being funny. It may be that it just wasn't laugh-out-loud funny, or was mildly amusing, or they didn't get it. But as long as you didn't laugh first, then the awkward moment does not occur. Rule one of comedy: don't laugh before your audience does.

Especially avoid trying to be esoterically funny. Do you know what I mean by this? I know many people who assume everyone gets the obscure reference they make in a joke. This is fine with your friends, but a stranger is just going to find it odd and often uncomfortable. You are hiding behind a mask of comedy rather than just being human; being human works much better. Using an obscure reference to show how knowledgeable you are also falls into the territory of being a know-it-all. So, you're breaking two principles.

Maybe even three. Introducing humor creates a "Top This" tension in the conversation. So, let the other person be funny, and you add a little to it. Or just compliment them on how funny they are.

Finally, attempting humor early on is going to make it much harder to relax, because comedy is a higher-risk interaction.

In short, don't try to be so clever or witty right out of the gate. Let's face it, not everyone has your sense of humor. Some people don't have any at all. But being droll, witty, snarky, clever, glib, or ironic are all very specific shades of humor, and when someone is not expecting it or attuned to that type of humor, and you try to roll out those shades of subtlety, you are lowering your odds of positive reception or even comprehension. Dial it back to being friendly and finding a common ground. Communication is about being understood, not making sounds.

DON'T EMBED A HIDDEN BIAS

Especially at the outset, avoid embedding some personal bias into an initial conversation. Political and religious views should be approached with caution. If you have a strong bias or opinion in these areas, know that it will put many people off. Gender bias is also another one.

Racial or ethnic biases are, too, obviously. If you can't start a conversation without injecting one of those, then please, shut the hell up. Like, permanently. My advice is to stay shy and stay home until you decide to evolve.

Also, when asking a question, be careful not to let your personal biases color your words. Political bias is a typical example, as in, "Can you believe what the president said last night?" You may eventually realize they are a kindred spirit, or one of your tribe, and you can loosen up. But don't kick off the conversation that way.

Sometimes you have to stop the first two or three things that come into your head from coming out of your mouth. This is a good reflex to not just speak without some—wait for it—Preparation. You'll get better, but often the first few things you come up with aren't ideal.

Let me illustrate with something that happened to me. I was riding in a taxi in Las Vegas, right after Donald Trump was elected. After the usual exchange of niceties, my driver said, "I'm pretty happy about the direction this country is going in."

To which I replied, "I'm very interested in seeing what Mr. Trump does." (Do you see how I tried to stay neutral?)

Then the cab driver said, "At least he's going to send those wetbacks back where they belong." Wow. Talk about embedding your bias. Not knowing me at all, he made three assumptions: first, I'm white, so therefore I must hate immigrants. Second, I must be an extreme right-wing Republican. And third, I'm going to be comfortable with racial slurs. Wrong on all three counts.

This is an extreme example to point out how quickly people can assume things that aren't necessarily true and reveal their ugly side. This guy never read *How to Make Friends and Influence People*, that's for sure.

I engage in heated political discussions with my friends all the time. But I already know their basic positions and beliefs. And as far as racial or ethnic slurs, people who use them are not my friends. The Boldness Exercises are about initial encounters, so proceed with much greater caution and don't make the assumption that everyone thinks like you or believes what you do. In fact, I can guarantee you that a whole bunch of people don't. Remember the prime directive. Do you think that cab driver made me feel good about myself? He made me sad that someone would even think and talk the way he did.

DON'T EAVESDROP

Eavesdropping generally falls into the "creepy" category. Or at least the weird category. Unless you can clearly overhear someone trying to find out something innocuous that you know, like directions, don't interject something. Or if you are truly trying to protect them from some type of danger or grievous mistake. In fact, those two things are pretty much the entire list of acceptable reasons to jump in based on eavesdropping.

First of all, it tells them you were listening to their private conversation, which in public is considered, at the very least, discourteous by most people. It is a mistake to feel like you are invited into the conversation just because you can hear it.

Granted, you may be on an airplane and can't shut out the conversation. But don't invite yourself in by adding to what you overheard. The only polite way into the conversation is to say, "I couldn't help but overhear that you _____" (just got back from Paris/had open heart surgery/found a dolphin in your swimming pool). And then ask a question.

Or you can say something, but not based on what you overheard. If they invite you in after you initiate with another topic, that is the moment when you can perhaps say, "I couldn't help but hear that you had dinner at Nobu in Hollywood last night. Did you see any movie stars?"

Now you might say, "Fred, I thought that inherent in the concept of boldness was *not* respecting people's privacy." No. Interrupting people who are having a private conversation that you can clearly tell is private is rude. The essential difference here is finesse. If there is an opening or opportunity, then take it—but not in a bizarre, rude, creepy, or stalker-ish way.

I'm definitely also saying check yourself to see if you're using "respecting privacy" as an excuse. You'll learn to assess yourself and the situation with practice. My point is that you need to be keenly aware of when eavesdropping crosses the line. If in doubt, always come down on the side of caution.

As always, if you've made an advance, a volley, and it's not returned, don't keep pushing it. Learn the signals and learn to respect that person's lack of interest. You have no idea where their headspace is. They could be in the middle of a divorce, or a work deadline, or falling in love, or late for an appointment, or just grumpy, or hormonal. Don't take it personally. Respect their privacy willingly if they've indicated that's what you should do.

Then there's a variation of this behavior, which sometimes involves eavesdropping and other times just involves wedging yourself into a conversation. This is also something to be cautious with, especially if it involves just two people. If it's a party and a few people are idly chatting, then it's perfectly acceptable to introduce yourself. But outside of that type of social situation, it's more challenging and also somewhat inconsiderate, especially if it looks like the two people are engaged seriously in a conversation.

If you find yourself saying, "I hate to interrupt, but..." this is the clue that you are wedging yourself into a conversation. Plus, you're lying. You wouldn't be interrupting if you hated to do it. It's a dumb way to start. Avoid the wedge move. Exceptions would be, as I mentioned: at a party, or also in a bar or club, where it is presumed that people are there to meet people. Then you'd be better off saying, "May I join you?" and give them the space to turn you down. And don't walk away hurt. Give them a polite smile and move on.

Especially don't wedge into a conversation and try to interject your observations at the same time you're interrupting someone. You can walk up and say, "That's a fascinating thing you just said. May I join into this brilliant exchange, or would you prefer to continue in private?" Odds are they admire the way you approached, but also, don't be hurt if they take you at your word. They may be old friends who haven't seen each other in years. Allow them to be candid. Don't read into it. Move on.

As an aside, the concept of "working the crowd" implies that you are out to gain something. That, to me, is the wrong attitude with which to approach a group of people. That's having an agenda. Instead, I would break the group down into individuals and focus on them one at a time. You're not working anybody. You're being human.

BREAKING THE PHYSICAL BARRIER

Making physical contact with someone you've just met is a touchy issue, if you'll forgive the pun. There are certainly many situations where you can touch someone. It's easy to touch people in a nonsexual way—on the shoulder, or the back or arm—but you need to be sensitive to everyone's tolerance of it. There are also many situations where physical contact can make people uncomfortable if they perceive it the wrong way, or if it's too soon, in their mind.

What is absolutely critical is that your intention has to be innocent, meaning that you are simply touching them as a human being, not as a sexual prospect.

This, of course, is different if you are on a date or meeting someone and trying to further the interaction to a point of intimacy. But I'm not talking about that. I'm talking about just breaking the physical barrier to put people at ease. This only works when you come from a place devoid of ulterior motive. Otherwise, you will often see it in the person's face, or they will actually recoil from your touch.

Be very aware of when you have crossed this boundary and it is unwelcome. Give them space. Apologize, even. Say, "Excuse me, I'm kind of a touchy person. Please forgive me." And back up a foot or two.

The same is true even for a handshake. You can hold it too long, and it gets weird. Hugging is a whole other level. Knowing when someone wants a hug is an art. I know people who can sense when it's appropriate and they do it all the time. But it's always because people don't feel there's anything creepy about it. I've become a hugger myself, but I'm always sensitive about people's space and particular attitude toward physical contact.

A hug from someone you've just met and talked to for a while is actually a great indicator of how open and vulnerable you were in the conversation and how connected they feel toward you. You'll experience it more and more as you refine your boldness. Just don't push it.

THE SCAM APPROACH

There are some techniques being taught on how to meet people, particularly on how to pick up women, that I don't subscribe to. Not that they don't work, it's just that there is a bit of a con artist approach to many of them. I'm trying to make boldness a life skill for you and have it affect every aspect of your life. I view these other techniques as manipulative rather than genuine. I also question the goal, which is often to seduce someone rather than create a real relationship.

But these approaches demonstrate something very important to understand, and that is that most people are approachable. To illustrate, let me relate an interaction I overheard at my local Starbucks.

I watched a young man approach a young woman who was working on her computer, and he struck up a conversation based on offering her a free training program at a gym he belonged to. He wasn't even very smooth in his pitch, but she was young and naive enough not to have a functioning BS detector. Within a few minutes, he was telling her she was going to meet rich guys, good-looking guys, and movie industry guys at this gym. He added this because she indicated she had moved to LA to become an actress.

But what happened then was remarkable. She was actually interested in the gym membership, and he told her that the benefit to him was he got more free membership time for everyone he got to take the free trial. Very little of what he was saying was true, and she could have easily gotten the free membership month without his help. But then he asked for her phone number, AND SHE GAVE IT TO HIM! Without any hesitation whatsoever, I might add.

Now, I'm totally against the fictional-story scam approach, but the point is, it worked. And this guy was beyond weird, and she would have been classified as being way out of his league—except within five minutes he had her cell number. Then he quickly pinned her down as to what day she was going to try the gym and told her he would call her and let her know she was on the list, and you can bet he will show up at the same time she does. And that won't be the only thing he calls about.

Creepy? Maybe. I go back to my point: on her, at least, it worked. The simple truth is that most people are approachable and generally trusting, despite what you've been telling yourself. I prefer an honest encounter rather than a scam approach. But if this guy can make a dishonest approach work, then surely you can come up with an honest one.

This pickup artist's primary life skill is that he isn't concerned about the encounter going wrong. He just proceeds with confidence. He doesn't say to himself, "I don't want to come off as creepy," and stop himself. He goes directly for the girl's phone number. Now, she may eventually find him unappealing, and I expect she will, sooner rather than later, but you never know.

Two key lessons: 1. People are surprisingly approachable, and 2. Don't create a scam-type approach. Be genuine.

DON'T BE CREEPY

This principle is primarily for the males. For God's sake, don't be creepy. And please develop a keen sense of what that would be. Creepy is a female code word for "person to avoid/sleazeball/stalker/potential rapist." So, talking about her body parts in the first sentence or two (unless you're in a nightclub at 1:00 a.m. and everyone is drunk) is creepy. Looking at those body parts instead of their eyes while you're talking to them is also creepy. Making some sexually suggestive joke right at the outset is creepy. Most of the time, touching them in the first sentence or two can venture toward creepy, as well.

Men, on the other hand, generally don't find women creepy. This is not a big problem for us. But men can be phenomenally creepy. I know men who have been creepy at work, never mind out in the general public. Creepy leads nowhere. Creepy sticks to you. Avoid it like the plague that it is.

Here's your first clue that you are delusional about your lack of creepiness. If you think saying something suggestive means the woman will be flattered that you find her sexually attractive, you are dead wrong. This may work in a pickup situation, but it doesn't start any sort of real relationship. It objectifies the woman, and if she responds positively, guess what? She's objectifying you too. You are serving a temporary purpose for her, and she's no more interested in really knowing you than you are her. Good luck with that.

Other lines to avoid in the first few moments of a conversation:

"Where are you from?" You are implying that they are not from your city, or state, or country. This is something that may come up later, but as an opener it sounds a lot like "You don't belong here" or "You seem different," without indicating if that's good or bad in your mind. Racist or prejudiced is its own special type of creepy.

The worse variation of this is "What's your ethnicity?" Often this is phrased even more poorly, as in "What are you, Oriental?" You can fill in the blank with any antiquated or offensive term for a suspected race/ethnicity/country of origin.

"When are you due?" Most people know this, but never assume a woman is pregnant. Not ever. This isn't creepy so much as deeply obtuse.

"Are those real?" Whether you are referring to teeth, breasts, or hair plugs, this is always a bad idea. It objectifies the person down to their component parts, and you're on your way to creepy.

DON'T BE WEIRD

Many people who are socially challenged have ways of compensating, often by trying to come up with things that make them unique. Most of the time, those things are just weird. Don't invent what you think are catch phrases that make you unique—like instead of saying hello, you say, "Top o' the morning to ya!" or "How are you this *belle matin*?" Don't be afraid to be normal, to be mundane, to be trite, even. What do people who barely know each other talk about? The weather. Does it kill them to do it? Do they think the other person is weird or strange or too inquisitive or invading their space? No. Its virtue is its very harmlessness, its lack of intrusiveness.

There is nothing wrong with blending. By that I mean not trying to stand out or be unique, but to focus on the other person and make them feel interesting. You're actually striving for that. There is time enough to be unique. You're not sacrificing any part of your personality (despite the story you're telling yourself right now) by being sociable in a conventional way.

You don't become bold by pretending to be someone else or by inventing behaviors that mask your shyness. You do it by defeating under-confident behavior in favor of boldness.

There is a fine line between unique and odd. But like the old line about pornography, we know weird when we see it. It's OK to be quirky, unique, and have your own style, but check yourself to see if it's something you're hiding behind. If you really like *World of Warcraft*, then those will be your people, and it will be hard to weird them out. But do you really need to narrow your social spectrum that much? Or are you hiding again?

When you don't think you can fit into a specific social circle, the tendency is to rebel against it, dismissing it as a group you're not interested in. I'm hoping your desire is that you can decide at any given moment what tribe you'd like to blend in with and be able to do it. You will always have your favorite tribe, but it's a big world. Why not get out there and enjoy all of it?

CHAPTER 17

WHAT YOU'RE MISSING OUT ON

Our lack of confidence, reticence, and hesitance (all part of the same unbold behavior) cause us to miss out on some really good things in life.

For example, unbold people often hate travel, especially places that don't speak their native language. The idea of a foreign country scares them. They have enough trouble with people who speak English, never mind people who don't. Having to ask strangers for directions, or trying to order food? Terrifying.

For bold people, it's all part of the fun. They embrace the chaos, and love when they finally get something to eat after a lot of confusing effort. They get lost in a cab and discover the most amazing little neighborhood that they would have never gone to. Bold people let random stuff happen and allow unexpected things to be discovered, and their lives are enriched immeasurably as a result.

We also miss out when our reticence keeps us from telling people what we expect from them. Whether it's at work, or in our relationship, or with our children, we hesitate to express what we expect in return when we do something, in the hope that the person will respond the way we want them to.

Expecting people to read our minds is wishful thinking. Most of the time, whoever you're dealing with would much rather have you spell out what's expected of them. This is true with employees, spouses, and children.

Imagine never speaking up to your mate when you wish they would be affectionate, and then resenting them for not doing it. They may believe that they are giving you what you want—a comfortable home, a well-cooked meal, a companion to watch TV with. How can they know if you don't say? And how many relationships spiral downward because of these unexpressed desires?

Imagine a child who gets everything they want, without a parent ever saying what they expect the child to do for themselves or the household? These children grow up feeling entitled to everything, not realizing that the world does not feel the same obligation as their parents did.

Speaking up isn't easy. It's just incredibly important.

The following are some life skills that will develop as you master boldness.

COLLABORATION

Here's another thing: under-confidence and reticence are not helping you at work, because you don't like to collaborate. Unbold people hate collaborating. We like to do things all by ourselves. Is that so bad? Only when you think about the power of collaboration in comparison. Lennon and McCartney were never better than when they were together. Elton John never wrote a single lyric to his songs; Bernie Taupin did. Steve Jobs started Apple with Steve Wozniak. And NASA put a man on the moon with the largest scientific collaboration in history.

As uncomfortable as it is, the risk of exposing your ideas to someone else often pushes you to be better. But also, the best results often come from collaboration. Agile programming teams are a perfect example. Art directors and copywriters working together in ad agencies is another. Each individual brings strengths and weaknesses, and together they compensate for each other and elevate the end result. In fact, Google considers the most important personality trait when hiring to be how well a person works as a member of a team.

Even worse, the less bold you are, the more reluctant you are to ask people for help. This is a giant impediment to success. Whether it be at work, creating a business, doing art, learning a musical instrument, or completing a personal project, if you are unwilling to seek guidance, support, input, or feedback, you lose out.

What happens is you won't do your best work, or you don't learn and grow as fast as you could. But much worse is when you won't even *start* something because you know it would require you to ask for help. You could hold your entire career back this way, or your marriage, or your personal art, or never start a business of your own.

"I prefer to work alone," is another way of saying, "I'm afraid to submit my work to any scrutiny until I have it perfect." This is a common behavioral aspect of unboldness. You don't want to have your ideas heard or seen until you're ready. But collaborators trust each other, don't judge each other, and make each other and the end product better. The proof is everywhere.

If you're not good at collaborating, you're holding yourself back at work. No doubt about that. Team player? Doesn't sound like it. Promotions will be few and far between.

You're also missing out on the joy of accomplishing something as part of a team, with having people to share in the glory of the achievement. It's a wonderful and fulfilling thing to experience.

But maybe you are an author or a painter. Some things are by definition done alone. But the greatest writers have an array of friends and researchers who read their material and give them feedback, and also have serious, highly skilled editors they trust to make their work better. Painters have gallery owners who tell them what will sell and make it possible for them to earn a living painting. Musical artists often create by themselves but rely on other people—studio musicians, editors, producers, and engineers—to make their work better. The most successful ones are willing to submit themselves to merciless criticism.

Adele, perhaps one of the most brilliant and gifted writer/performers alive today, showed the initial songs of her third album, 25, to famed record producer Rick Rubin, who had produced her previous work to great success. Instead of saying, "These are fantastic, Adele, can I please produce these songs?" Rick, after listening to the demos, said simply, "I don't believe them." Adele could have said, "Hey, pal, my last album sold a trillion copies. I don't need your negativity." Instead, she took his critique to heart and went back and wrote a whole new batch of songs. I hear 25 did pretty well. Over 30 million copies worldwide.

Collaboration is the pathway to greater success. Almost nothing is accomplished by someone all by themselves. Bold people ask for help. All the time. For anything. Sometimes even if they don't need it, just because they want companionship along the way.

Finally, the more your work requires you to be alone, the more you need an effective social outlet. Rather than debate this further, I'll let it happen in the course of developing your boldness, and you can see for yourself.

SAYING NO

Being bold also means being comfortable *refusing* to help people. Unbold people are often afraid to tell someone no. Whatever the reason, we don't like to turn anyone down, because we hate the idea that someone would turn us down if we finally put ourselves out there and took some risk. That's what terrifies us, and therefore we don't want to be someone who does that to someone else. So we go along with everything. We do things we'd rather not because we lack the boldness to refuse. How twisted is that?

Then it goes deeper than that. We don't stand up for things that matter to us, that we object to. We create a pattern of going along even when we disagree. We're against shoplifting, but we let a friend get away with it. We find ethnic jokes objectionable, but we don't speak up and say so when someone tells one. We just laugh as we lose a little more respect for ourselves. We disagree with someone's politics, but pretend we agree to fit in. (I have dear friends who hate my political views. It just adds to the fun of the relationships!)

Bold people say no all the time. They are in fact stingy with their time, because they have big goals and they know what it takes to reach them. When they feel strongly about something, they say so. That's a pretty healthy place to come from. And they're extremely comfortable expressing their lack of desire to do something. Wouldn't you like that ability too? Wouldn't that feel great?

Here's an apropos quote by author Jules Renard: "The truly free man is he who can decline a dinner invitation without giving an excuse."

BE THE ONE WHO ACTS

When you are afraid of strangers, you will eventually find yourself in a situation where you are hesitant to help someone in need. It may be someone in obvious distress, like a person lost and disoriented, or even injured. But because of under-confidence or potential embarrassment, you choose inaction. Time to change that choice.

One time, a friend of mine noticed a woman who seemed to be wandering the streets aimlessly in his neighborhood. He approached her and quickly discovered that she was suffering from Alzheimer's and had wandered out unnoticed from the family home where she was staying. He gently offered to escort her down the street, and she was delighted to find a gentleman with such good manners. He eventually saw a passing police cruiser that was on the lookout for her and flagged them down, and she got home safely.

Most people would likely have done nothing when faced with the same situation.

I recently was parking at a restaurant, and as I climbed out of my car, I noticed a woman and her elderly mother working their way up the incline of the driveway, which then led to a downward staircase and a walkway to the entrance. I stepped up and offered my arm to the elderly woman, and she hooked right onto me. She and her daughter spoke Spanish, so I didn't really understand the exchange between them (it was a Cuban restaurant), but I'm pretty sure she wasn't saying, "I wish this oddball would leave me alone."

She thanked me as I led her in through the front door, and I walked to the counter to pick up my takeout order. And you know what? It felt just plain fantastic to do it. The younger me would have had a dozen reasons not to do it: "I'm in a hurry"; "She might think I'm weird"; "Someone else will do it," all of them stupid rationalizations. I have offered many an elderly woman my arm and never been refused.

I have walked up to several people over the years who appeared lost. Not all of them were, but those who were showed great appreciation for my helpfulness. The only true upside to xenophobia is that you keep yourself from encountering a serial killer. Considering the odds of that are about 50 million to 1, then you're at much greater risk driving in your car all by yourself, where your risk of dying in a crash is 1 in 10,000 in any given year. Relax about the serial killers. You watch too much TV.

And really, what could be worse than being too hesitant to perform an act of kindness?

Imagine a more drastic situation, where someone trips and falls and injures themselves. Or they get in a car accident. Are you going to let your hesitance stop you from stepping up? I hope not. I hope that the Boldness Exercises will make you the first one to act, instead of the last.

I recently flew on a Southwest Airlines flight. It was a very light passenger load, only forty people, and I happened to be the first regular passenger on the plane. I had seen a mother walk her young daughter onto the plane ahead of me, after hearing an announcement for an unaccompanied minor. Which meant the mother was leaving her daughter on the plane by herself. When I got on the plane, I saw the girl, who was no more than eight years old, alone, sobbing in her window seat.

I was going to sit in the bulkhead row in front of her, but I looked at her and said, "Don't be sad," and then I decided I would sit in the aisle seat next to her. I asked her if she wanted to play a game on my iPad, and she nodded. I moved to the empty middle seat to set her up with the game, and then asked if that was her mother who had brought her on the plane, and she said, in a fragile voice, "Yes, I was visiting her, and now I'm flying back to be with my dad."

She was still sniffling, but once I got her playing *Angry Birds*, she seemed to calm down. We talked about the game, and then the plane moved away from the gate and she was looking out the window, so I left her my iPad and slid back over to the aisle seat. (I know there is this ever-present fear of pedophiles now, but I was damned if I was going to let that control my behavior. Let people have their judgments and paranoia.) As we began to taxi out of the gate, I simply told her, "I'm going read for a while. You can use my iPad as long as you want."

She quickly fell asleep. Then, unfortunately, we had mechanical trouble and had to go back to the gate and deplane. We waited in the gate area, and then finally switched planes and boarded again, feeling like we were in the movie *Groundhog Day*. This time a flight attendant brought the girl on board and was with her in the bulkhead aisle. I resumed my seat a row back.

As they boarded the plane, a ground crew member came in with a walkie-talkie and told the girl that her mother was going to come onto the plane to talk to her. After several minutes, it was transmitted that the mother had gone outside TSA security and could not get back through, and so she wasn't going to be able to come on board and talk to her daughter, but she was going to call her. Then the flight attendant asked the girl for her cell phone. Unfortunately (and bizarrely, in my mind, making me question her parents' judgment and priorities), she didn't have a cell phone. So, I stood up and said to the crew person, "Have her mother call my phone number," and handed her my cell. She then used the walkie-talkie to give my number to the person outside security, who told the mother.

My phone rang, and I handed it to the girl. She talked to her mother and, in the course of the conversation, let on that she wanted to get off the plane and stay with her mother, which her mom agreed to and finally they took the girl off the plane.

The flight attendant, Mary, thanked me for my help.

The reason I tell you this story is twofold. Many people wonder why, when certain crimes or situations are witnessed, that no one steps up and does something. In particular, there was a story in the 1980s about a woman who was being attacked outside a New York apartment building, and everyone in the building could hear her screaming for help. Many even looked out their windows. But no one called the police.

This nonresponse is often repeated in a variety of situations, so some psychologists did a study on the phenomenon. They found out that if the person witnessing the situation were alone, then they would act. But if there were a number of people watching, they would all hesitate to be the first one to take action. In the case of the woman who was attacked in front of the building, everyone assumed that someone else had already called the police.

The first reason I'm telling you this is because you don't want to fall into the trap of thinking that someone else will act. Someone's life could be at stake, or some child could be left sobbing by herself when everyone is wondering why no one consoles her. You don't want to fall victim to this assumption. And you don't ever want a lack of boldness to keep you from being the one to act when it matters.

Remember, just being a bystander doesn't make you innocent. A lot of people choose to just stand by and watch, but it doesn't relieve them of a moral obligation or even a social one simply because other people didn't act either.

The second reason is that there is tremendous satisfaction in being the one who acts. This may be one of the most important reasons to cultivate boldness. It is quite likely that your action, your bold behavior, will matter very much to someone else, and you will feel gratification instead of guilt or regret. And, perhaps most importantly, you will feel the connection to another human being, one to whom you acted charitably, expecting nothing in return. When you discover how deeply satisfying that can be, you will never miss the opportunity to do so. Your life will be genuinely fulfilling, I promise you, in ways you never imagined.

CHAPTER 18

SPECIAL SITUATIONS AND BOLD SKILLS

APOLOGIZING

One afternoon with a group of friends, I did something — a vulgar prank—trying to be funny, and to me it was, but it was kind of stupid and potentially embarrassing to the person I did it to. I will not describe the action, but let's just say that the average person would not be amused. But this person, though surprised, laughed and said, "Fred, you are not right in the head!"

Almost immediately I sensed my inappropriateness, or at least the possibility that this person didn't really appreciate the prank.

Now, the old Fred would have just carried it around the rest of his life as a memory to be uncomfortable about. But instead, an hour later, I sought this person out and apologized. He dismissed my apology as totally unnecessary, and he actually did think it was funny.

So, I could have made the lesson: "See? I don't have to apologize for the stupid things I do." But that wasn't the point because I felt radically better immediately after apologizing, and now I don't have to carry that gut-twisting memory. If the person indeed had been embarrassed or offended, then it would have been even better to have apologized. Either way, I win by apologizing.

I have dozens of things in my past that I wish I'd apologized for. I imagine most of us do. But I've finally stopped accumulating them. Whenever possible, I find that person who was my "victim" in the past. I remind them of the incident, and I apologize for it. Most of the time, they don't even remember. But when they do, and if it did bother them, they are very grateful that I sought them out and apologized. It makes me proud of myself.

Apologizing sincerely is a life skill. Yet many of us, myself included, have this peculiar feeling that we are losing something, some part of our esteem or stature, when we apologize. When you are not confident, when you have not truly harnessed boldness, then that may be true. But a bold person doesn't lose any self-esteem by apologizing when they know— or even suspect—that they were wrong. They in fact gain self-esteem because they know that the apology is the exact behavior they want to do, without hesitation.

And you won't have to carry around the regret. That's a big bonus.

TRYING EMOTIONS ON FOR SIZE

Growing up shy, I was so bad at expressing my emotions that I had grown completely out of touch with them. When someone would ask me what I was feeling, most of the time I couldn't connect with myself enough to adequately describe it, never mind vocalize it. But as I moved beyond my shy behavior, I started to get better at expressing myself, and eventually it became possible to identify the emotions I was feeling.

I could always feel anger pretty easily because I was angry about a lot of things, and of course it demanded to be released. But subtler emotions, like sadness, or empathy, or gratitude, all escaped me, so I had to develop an awareness of them. I learned a trick from a great teacher, Christine Price, who taught me many things at Esalen Institute about connecting to my emotions.

The trick is this: sometimes you have to express a feeling verbally just to see if it feels true. Saying it out loud is the proving ground for yourself. You don't have to be certain of your exact emotion ahead of time. You're trying it on for size, so to speak, to see if it might be accurate.

For example, let's say someone in your family that you were not particularly close to passes away, and you find you can't really summon any sadness about the loss. But you liked the person, maybe even loved them. So, find a quiet place alone and say out loud, "I'm really sad about Aunt Rita" or "I'm really going to miss her." Say it a few times, and then see how it feels. Does it stir something in you? Does it feel genuine? Maybe, maybe not. Try something else if it doesn't, like, "I feel guilty that I didn't call her that often."

Remember, no one is going to hear you. You are trying it on for size. This process of vocalizing triggers a different part of your brain, and it may start to release the true emotion. The goal is to see what resonates, then become better at both connecting to your emotions and expressing them.

Another example might involve someone getting promoted instead of you. You may say, "I'm really angry about her getting that job. I deserved it." But that's going for the easy emotion. Are you really angry? Maybe you're actually disappointed. Or maybe you're disappointed in yourself for not working harder. Try a different emotion on for size than the default anger response. Maybe you're just envious. Try that on and see if it fits.

You can even try something that you don't believe is accurate at all, just to see how it feels. You could say, "I'm happy she got the job" or "I'm proud of her." And then see how that feels. You may end up saying, "No, that's not it." You tried it on, and it didn't fit. That's good to know too. Do this exercise when someone can't hear you, but do it out loud, at least three times. You'll be surprised by what other layers of emotion you can uncover.

You may find you feel several things at once. In the last example, you could probably feel a combination of jealousy, anger, resentment, depression, disappointment, and maybe even a hint of happiness for the other person. In fact, seldom are we feeling just one thing.

But wouldn't it be nice to identify and express those emotions? That's one of the most precious things that boldness can do for you, is connect you to your feelings and make you able to express them accurately and articulately. Do we not envy people who can do that? Then say it out loud, "I envy bold people!" Does that feel accurate?

One of the essential elements of a fulfilling life is to be able to express your deepest feelings to someone close to you, whether it's your partner, a parent, a child, or a dear friend. Your reticence often goes into such high gear at this point that you can't even formulate your thoughts in order to express them. The Boldness Exercises are going to clear your mind of the debris blocking you and give you the boldness to talk about things that really matter, at a time when they matter most. It could save your marriage, or protect a friend, or just let someone know how much you care, or help them to truly understand you. This particular technique will make it possible to identify exactly what you're feeling.

Bold people will often try emotions on for size right in front of people and examine if they're true or not. If it doesn't resonate, they'll just correct it and say, "No, that's not true; what I really feel is disappointment." That's where you eventually want to get to. People are perfectly comfortable with you changing your mind, and they even admire you for being willing to expose your emotional process openly.

SEXUALLY SHY

If reading about sexual behavior makes you uncomfortable, don't read this next part. (That warning label pretty much guarantees that everyone will read on!)

Sex is a touchy subject in a relationship. There are people who have been married for thirty years and never suggested to their mate to try a different sexual position. Even if the woman doesn't climax in the one position they've been using for three decades, she doesn't bring it up. There are people who indeed have never climaxed at all with their partners, who fake it, who dismiss it as unimportant.

I realize there is a whole other layer of inhibition going on once you enter the sexual arena. The risk of shame, embarrassment, and rejection skyrockets, and the longer the relationship goes on, the harder it is, so to speak, to bring up changes. And so, your sex life declines. Or worse, one person starts looking elsewhere. Maybe they don't look elsewhere for sex; maybe they are just seeking attention or affection. But very often they are seduced by someone who is more open, or open-minded, or just more sexually experienced.

This reticence with respect to sex is clearly a lack of boldness. Sadly, most people say that it's much easier to ask for what you want from a sexual partner that you barely know than it is with your mate. It makes sense, though, because there is a lot less risk.

What also happens is one person has taboos or restrictions that they express early in the relationship. If your husband has made it clear that oral sex is out of the question, then the woman is unlikely to feel any obligation to reciprocate. If your husband is fast asleep moments after his climax, many wives hesitate to suggest that perhaps he might spend a minute or two bringing her to orgasm, or maybe to a second one. So, they slide into the mundane, routine sex that eventually leads to none at all.

Does this make you uncomfortable reading about this? That's your first clue that you're sexually shy. None of us would be here if it weren't for sex. Yet we can't talk about it.

How ridiculous is this trap? Wouldn't it be incredibly satisfying to inject some honesty and candor into our sex lives? To get some satisfaction out of it and feel more connected to the person? And get our needs met? God forbid we get our needs met in a close relationship. Isn't that why you got together in the first place?

It's that same fear of rejection, which is irrational and missing the point. Because the point is to enjoy sex. Dolphins do, and you can too. (Dolphins, by the way, are the only other mammals besides humans that have sex purely for enjoyment—and they don't have any hang-ups about it!) Face it, there are people in prison having sex more than you. Not always willingly but, nevertheless, why would you want to lose *that* competition?

What would the worst result be if you started to communicate about your desires? Less sex? You're already headed in that direction. That's the irrational part. You're worried that you're going to lose something that is already slipping away on its own. And maybe, if you get clear on it, the other person will surprise you and be honest too, and you may actually find out what is keeping you from making it a priority and heightening your intimacy.

Sex is good for your brain, your sense of well-being, and your self-esteem. And your prostate, if you're a man. It's been proven over and over, and yet we let ourselves get bored, or get frustrated, or bring a bunch of baggage into bed. Or watch TV or scroll Instagram.

Here is a situation where Dosage is critical. This is going to take baby steps. Don't go revealing your S&M fantasies right away, because in fact they may fade when you start to get regular sex. We tend to get wilder and kinkier in our fantasies than what we actually would like to participate in. How about suggesting the favorite time of day you would like sex? Or asking when your partner would like sex and compromising even though you don't like morning sex that much. Making someone else feel good and happy isn't the worst result of a compromise, especially if this is supposedly the person closest to you.

It really starts with the simple question, "What do you enjoy?" Very often, the person doesn't have an answer. Or would very much like you to figure it out for them, either because of a lack of experience or their own inhibitions. So gentle prodding is in order.

Sometimes your partner may say, "I don't feel like having sex today." There could be all sorts of stress reasons, hormonal causes, or just fatigue. But if the reason is sexual boredom, you should want to fix it. Don't get upset. We all have our moods. But maybe you can ask, "Do you mind if I masturbate?" This question usually opens up a Pandora's Box of inhibitions. Be bold and see where it takes you. No one is going to die from this conversation, and your sex already is lackluster, so expect some bumps and grinds along the way as you try to improve it.

What's it like on the other side of this, which is sexual boldness? I can tell you that there are many people who know how to ask for exactly what they want in the sexual part of their relationships, without any hesitance or fear of rejection. They will say, "Feel free to spank me," as easily as asking for more cream in their coffee.

"But it ruins the mood, the spontaneity, to ask, doesn't it?" Sure, if you let it. But it's not the only time you're going to have sex, hopefully, so you're really trying to improve the next time and the time after that. Sooner or later, you have to do the hard thing and find a way to ask for what you want.

I'm no sex therapist, but I'll point out what should be obvious. If you can't verbalize what you want, what chance do you have of a sustainable sex life with that person? The result will be no sex from not speaking up, or no sex because they are unwilling to do what you want.

So why not take a chance and ask? If you don't ask, or you don't explain what appeals to you, then you are pretty much guaranteed not to get it. You should be asking them what they want and hopefully withholding judgment. Because asking that question may be more important than telling them what you want. And perhaps more difficult because of your reticence. So, take it slow. But if lack of sex is hurting your relationship, you better speak up.

And yes, I'm well aware of all the double entendres I slipped into this section. ;-)

TALKING TO SENIOR CITIZENS

I was visiting my elderly aunt in an assisted living facility, and I saw a teenager sitting in the visiting area with his white-haired grandfather. They weren't speaking to each other. The boy was fixated on his smartphone, while the old man stared at him. The man didn't look resentful, but rather seemed glad for the company, even though the boy was ignoring him.

But how sad that this boy did not know how to hold a conversation with an older person, one who clearly loved him and was in the last and loneliest years of his life. This is a skill we all need to master if we want to be truly decent human beings. It doesn't always have to be gratifying to you. What you gain is tangible, if not material. Why? Because someday you'll be old. And you don't want to be sitting there alone, being ignored, and saying to yourself, "Well, I guess I had this coming." The other reason, the better reason, is that living with a generous heart is the most fulfilling life of all.

Reticence should never keep you from simply talking to someone who is elderly. Tell them anything that comes in your head. My 101-year-old aunt was happy to talk about *anything*. I could tell her dirty jokes, and she would scold me and then ask for another. This is a gift you are giving yourself as well as the other person, and failing to develop this skill will leave you with a regret you might never be able to repair, because that person will be gone.

I now take this beyond my own family. If I see an older person, I greet them. I smile and say hello as I pass. I offer my arm if it seems necessary. I take half an hour out of my busy life and try to give them a little respite from their long, lonely days. I don't make excuses for myself so that I can escape. It's too easy, and it's too heartless, in the end.

Maybe you don't have to talk. Maybe just sit with them, not ignoring them. A few years ago, I watched the entire Super Bowl with my dying uncle, and we barely exchanged a word because he kept falling asleep and waking up. I didn't mind. He was just happy to have someone watching it with him.

If shyness, reticence, or lack of communication skills is keeping you from having a generous heart, then please use the PRIDE Method to change that. I can guarantee one thing in this book for certain, and that is that you will not ever regret the time you spent doing this.

ENCOUNTERING CELEBRITIES

There are also a few stumbles you can avoid along the way as you harness your boldness. They will happen mostly because you didn't do one of the PRIDE steps. One in particular is when you encounter a celebrity.

If you do see someone you recognize and genuinely admire, then this is an excellent boldness challenge. It will also have a higher likelihood of failure. Remember, celebrities are haunted by paparazzi and drooling fans. Show some respect, and don't drool.

Let's say you recognize an actor but can't remember her name. Do NOT go up to her and ask her who she is. I actually heard someone do this to the actress Andie McDowell when she was in the Nashville airport. She was extremely gracious the entire time, telling the person her name, while this person was extremely intrusive and clueless. In short, it was discourteous and ignorant.

Also, don't call them by their character's name from the movie or TV show you recognize them from. That seldom is appealing, and it doesn't count as knowing their name.

Here's a basic guideline: if you don't remember the celebrity's name, don't approach them. It's not a compliment and generally not appreciated.

If you do know their name (or managed to find it in a quick Google search), then approach. But don't address them by their first name (unless they are mononymous like Beyoncé or Sting—but don't worry, you will not get near either of them). Call them by their last name, starting with Mr. or Ms. That's the polite way.

Whatever you do, don't make a spectacle of their presence, drawing a crowd to them. Recognize that they still have a right to privacy, even though they are in public. And don't nervously monologue. Be nice. Be complimentary and don't be invasive. They are being polite if they talk to you. It's not the start of a beautiful friendship. Be brief and break away.

A simple "I really enjoyed your work in…" or "I so admire your work" will suffice. The more specific you can be, the better. Most of the time, they will thank you. Some, if they don't feel intruded upon, will ask your name and shake your hand. But don't expect it or demand it.

I once encountered the actor Titus Welliver, who recently starred in the series *Bosch*, going through airport security. I simply said to him, "Mr. Welliver?" And he turned and said, "Yes?"

I said, "Really terrific work you are doing on *Bosch*."

He smiled, shook my hand, and said, "Thanks very much. And thanks for watching."

And I walked away. I got to tell him how much I liked the show, didn't draw attention to him, and then left him alone. I'd like to think I made him feel good about himself. As in, the prime directive. I was an uplifting voice, not a drooling fan.

I've lived in Los Angeles since 1980, so I've met several celebrities over the years. I've seen Jay Leno say hi to people who pulled up in a car next to him, and I've seen Arnold Schwarzenegger give people the cold shoulder. It doesn't make Jay any nicer than Arnold. The situations were different. That's all.

You may want to take a picture with them, and they will let you know if that's all right or if it's not. Respect that. But never do this in restaurants while they're eating and don't *ever* bother them when they are with their children. As I said, they are plagued by paparazzi most of the time, and when it comes to their children, they are extremely protective, as you would be.

Don't expect them to do a selfie with you when a crowd is starting to gather because people noticed you approaching successfully. They are usually not looking to spend the afternoon signing autographs or taking pictures.

Also, you may think the selfie gives you some weird bragging rights that you "met" them, but it's not like you hung out with them or they know you. Personally, I would rather have a real conversation with Matt Damon or Chris Rock than have taken a hundred selfies with various celebrities but hadn't said or exchanged anything significant. But that's me.

When it's with a stranger, a selfie has become a way of acting as if you've had a real human connection. It's pretending to be friends. Sound judgmental? Maybe. But my goal is to move you beyond superficial experiences and get you into deeper, more fulfilling ones.

Lastly, if you happen to know you're going to meet a celebrity, be prepared. Research them, remind yourself of your favorite moment or scene with them. Even better if it's something that they're not well-known for.

On one occasion, I knew that I was going to be at a breakfast with a group of people where the invited guest was Tom Brokaw, the longtime newscaster and author. A friend of mine, who was a great admirer of Brokaw's, heard that I was going to meet him, and sent me a small article from a local newspaper that had an interesting story about Mr. Brokaw and a high school friend of his. He asked if I could show the article to Mr. Brokaw and have him sign it. I took the opportunity to do just that toward the end of the breakfast, and it stimulated a lively story about the background of the article. It clearly brought up fond memories for Mr. Brokaw, and he gladly signed the article.

But the big lesson for me was the difference it made in being prepared to meet him (although it was my friend who had prepared me). It made the whole experience much richer and more personal for everyone, and I felt I had a totally unique experience because of it.

Lesson learned.

So as much as possible, be prepared. Then relax. Don't be a freak. Take a breath. Talk like a normal person talking to a regular person. You'll be amazed at how much it's appreciated.

GIVING A EULOGY

Remember at the beginning of the book, when I said that one of the reasons that you should want to become bold is because you may have to give a eulogy for someone close to you? The PRIDE Method will have prepared you for this.

You will want to have something written, with the confidence to know that you will get through it. Or you may simply be at a funeral and they invite people to speak, even though you were not going to be giving the eulogy yourself. If you loved this person, or love the people who loved this person, get up and say something. If you sit there too long, you will miss the chance. It doesn't have to be a long speech, or articulate, or impressive. It has to be heartfelt, and that's all. It's not a performance. It could be a single sentence. But it's one of the more important moments of your life.

People will appreciate it and will be grateful to you for making the effort. You might cry as you give the eulogy. So what? No one will think any less of you. Most likely the opposite. Even if you're not sure there will be a chance to speak, prepare something. The times I didn't, I wished I had, because afterward I thought of exactly what I wanted to say. My advice is to think about it beforehand, write something, however simple and brief, and then use it as the foundation to speak from your heart. Step 1, Preparation.

I recently watched my cousin Paul give a eulogy for his mother, and in the middle of it he made a joke. That may seem inappropriate, but it was the relief everyone needed. He had spoken from the heart about how wonderful a woman his mother was, and the church was full of people who knew her and loved her. That moment of levity was something we all knew his mother would have enjoyed. But that's what you can do when you've cultivated boldness. I was proud of him, and I want you to be able to do the same thing when it matters most.

PART V

SUPERBOLDNESS

CHAPTER 19

SUPERBOLDNESS

"Be yourself. Everyone else is taken."

—Oscar Wilde

Superboldness happens when you bring all you've learned into your everyday life so that you can be as bold as you want, whenever you want.

Maybe you read the entire book before you started the Boldness Exercises. That's fine. Now do the exercises. Every damn day. And write about them in your journal. This will become essential to track your progress and to maximize the learning from each exercise.

The following are not exercises but activities that will address real issues in your life. They will put your boldness to the test and will build your boldness muscle in the same way. Because now it's for real.

DEFUSE YOUR CRINGEWORTHY MOMENTS

We all have our collection of cringeworthy moments. Most of mine are decades old. I rarely create a new one now. In your moments of nervousness or social unease, you undoubtedly have said or done things you wish you hadn't. These moments are destructive because they add fuel to Doctor No, who tells you that you are not good enough.

It doesn't matter how they happened; these moments make you cringe. Hopefully you have listed some of them in your journal because the way to begin to defuse these cringe bombs is to write them down, then go back and read them all out loud, and fully embrace the cringe. Eventually they just don't seem that significant, especially as you learn what to do instead.

Now I want you to do the next bold step. At this point, I want you to take some time after you've done some of the Boldness Exercises, at least to Level 3, and choose a cringeworthy moment where you are still in contact with the person or persons involved. Then, find them and ask them if they remember. If they do, apologize if necessary, and explain that you were a social misfit. Have a conversation about it.

If you do this and it was significant, and you manage to reflect and apologize to the person, they will look very kindly on the fact that you are perceptive enough to know that it was inappropriate but didn't know how to apologize back then.

Or, if you are relating the cringe moment to a good friend, they will most likely laugh and say, "Do you really think I care anymore? Or even remember it?" Or they could say, "Hey, we all say stupid shit that alienates people. Most of us don't even realize we're doing it. You at least do and want to fix it. Good for you."

Do this with as many of these moments as possible. All of them, ideally. Bring your cringeworthy moments to light so that they can wither and die in the bright sun.

You want to erase these so that, as you go forward, they are not putting the brakes on your boldness. You also want to learn from them, because the effect they had on you and the other person is the opposite of what you really wanted.

EMBRACE EMBARRASSMENT

This is the upside of doing something potentially embarrassing: no matter what, it's a win. What the heck am I talking about? Embarrassment feels terrible, right? Sure it does, unless you are OK with risking it. Then people admire you for not being devastated by it. In fact, in this activity, you are not truly embarrassed. You're just doing something deliberately that others—and the old you—might describe as embarrassing.

I once did a dance onstage in front of an audience of five thousand people, and I told myself that either way, whether I danced badly or well, they would be impressed because I was bold enough to attempt it. I couldn't lose, *unless I decided to judge myself.* Which I decided not to do. And, depending on who you were in the audience, I either embarrassed myself or impressed you. I wasn't going to get exactly the same reaction from everyone. That's impossible. But not minding either way was the key for me. Knowing that everyone got to have their own judgment made it pure fun.

Some audience members might have thought I was a show-off. Others might have called me a showman. I can live with either one because a whole lot of people had fun and got inspired, and that's what I was going for.

Also, if you accidentally do something embarrassing and you show people that you are fine with it, then you win. You win their admiration, and you don't call it a failure. You were just being a human being. We are all flawed, and most people dread embarrassment, but the fact is—Guiding Principle #8—Nothing. Bad. Happens.

Spill wine on your new dress? Say, "I wonder if Walmart will take this back?" Trip and fall? Say, "I'm glad my ballet teacher wasn't here to see that." (Works for both genders, by the way.) If you just roll with it, people will admire you instead of laughing at you or feeling sorry for you.

But every risk we take has the potential to be a failure, and every public or social risk we take could fail, and we could label it an embarrassment and indulge that feeling. Or we could acknowledge that playing it safe is not a choice we're willing to make anymore. Now, we're going to embrace the potential for embarrassment as part of the fun.

Think about something important to you, something that you would like to do, but you would have been too embarrassed to do before the Boldness Exercises and are still a little fearful about it. Give it a try and see if it even registers as something to be embarrassed about anymore.

ACT FOOLISH

Foolish is human. Perfection isn't. Foolish is vulnerable. Foolish is endearing. Aloof isn't. Foolish is real. You don't want to be "above" anyone, and you certainly don't want to project that.

At least once a week, and then maybe once a day, behave in a foolish, playful way, a way that you never would have before. Revel in it and delight in people's various reactions. Some of the Boldness Exercises are foolish, but I want these to be of your own design, something you personally want to act foolish about.

It may be wearing a costume to a party that you know is not a costume party. ("Oops, I misread the invitation!" Big grin.) It may be letting your eight-year-old nephew give you a haircut. It may be walking around with your fly down all day to see who tells you. It may be talking in a pirate accent all morning. It's up to you. But enjoy how much people actually enjoy your foolishness. It will be a revelation.

You may make some people uncomfortable. Acting foolishly, or silly, or comically, or overenthusiastically, will certainly make some people uncomfortable. But I can tell you that when you let go of that fear of judgment, it's absolutely liberating and joyful to act that way.

Now, when the situation presents itself, go completely off the rails a few times a month. Some of the Boldness Exercises incorporate this idea of foolishness, like singing karaoke badly, but I want you to pull out all the stops. Dive so deep into playing the fool that people won't recognize you. And revel in it.

SEEK OUT THE WALLFLOWER

Wallflowers. We've all seen them at company gatherings, or parties, or whatever event they may be at, and they end up sitting alone, or standing alone, or walking around looking at the artwork or music collection. It's painful for me to see, because I've been that person so often. But now I gravitate toward them almost uncontrollably. And I recommend you do the same.

This is like the Level 4 exercise, but I want this to become your modus operandi, not just for practice, but for real. Whenever you see this type of person, whatever the situation, make them your primary target. Walk right up to them and introduce yourself. Observe their behavior. Listen to them. Do they respond to questions and not ask the same of you? Do they not smile or make eye contact? When you finally get them engaged and opening up, do they monologue?

You're doing this in part to see how far you've come, but also as an act of kindness, to bring that person into the party or event, and pull them out of their hesitance and reticence, or outright shyness. Just as in the Boldness Exercise, you will politely excuse yourself at some point, as you have other people to meet. Later on, you'll invite them into a group conversation and introduce them.

Or perhaps you will invite other people into your conversation with the wallflower. Bold people do this all the time. They create a whole group conversation, and then they duck out and maybe start another one.

As I said, I do this now whenever the situation presents itself. It's gratifying and also a lot of fun. A lot more fun than being the wallflower was, I assure you.

GO DEEP

On your pathway to boldness, one of the stories your Doctor No will tell you is that you don't want to be some kind of social butterfly, flitting around the room at a party, meeting everyone, getting laughs and pats on the back, and everyone's smiling at you and talking about how wonderful it was to meet you, and how fabulous you are, and all that. You're not that superficial, your critic will say.

Well, to a degree, Doctor No will be right. That superficial experience can be nice, occasionally, and you want the ability to do it if you so choose. But on a regular basis, it does ring hollow. Which doesn't mean you don't interact. You will be doing something quite different than just that superficial pass through the room.

Your goal beyond the Boldness Exercises is to meet a number of people but go deep with two or three people at a party or event. In fact, I want you to be able to meet anyone you choose and be able to approach them and engage them in conversation, and then decide if you want to go deeper or not. If you do, then I want you to be able to take that conversation from the superficial to the meaningful. Find out what they really care about, what they may be hurting about, what they discovered about themselves or other people. This is going deep.

And that's a conversation worth having. You don't need ten of those at a party. You need one. And every once in a while, that person becomes someone special in your life, part of the inner circle that you're constructing for yourself.

But you know how it starts? With a superficial exchange. Almost no one is prepared to go deep in the first two or three sentences. Take your time.

One of the most powerful things you can do to effectively connect with people is to be vulnerable. When you tell someone something personal, a revelation that is not about your successes or accomplishments, but rather your doubts, your fears, or your failures, suddenly you become human to them. It also makes you appear humble to them, which, as a newly bold person, you will want to maintain.

This lesson came to me from Keith Ferrazzi, author of *Never Eat Alone*, in which he teaches a great strategy for meeting people and engaging them on a real level. He emphasizes the power of exposing your vulnerability as a way of dropping from a superficial and forgettable interaction to a true empathetic connection.

Shy people, of course, are terrified of exposing their vulnerabilities. "Talk about my vulnerabilities, my challenges, my failings?" Horrifying. Dangerous. Not doable.

Except what it really is, is disarming. That word is very appropriate because you are dropping your emotional armor. When someone is vulnerable, often you find that they reveal something about themselves that makes you realize they are like you, with their own frailties, baggage, and traumas.

As you grow in boldness, you will consciously decide that it is safe to be vulnerable, and people will find themselves doing the same with you. To get to those stories, that painful stuff, you will need to mine certain parts of your life, to explore what to reveal about yourself and your past. You may want to have a few things, varying in degrees of depth in your personal pain, so that you can control the Dosage of the situation. Your journal should be full of them by now.

I often tell people about how my mother had to take care of my brother, who had polio as a young child, and so, when I was very young, she would be gone for weeks at a time. Because I was so young, I completely detached emotionally from her and was never able to reconnect, however much we both tried.

Telling this to someone inevitably resulted in a deep conversation, and I found that it always had a profound effect on people. You are not just having a polite conversation but revealing something about yourself instead. That revelation opens the person to you, dropping the wall around you and dissolving the wall around them at the same time.

Sometimes vulnerability is a perfect way to introduce yourself to someone. Let's say you're at some gathering, doing a Level 2 Boldness Exercise. (Or just at a party.) You could say, "Hi, I'm Fred, and I don't know anyone here. I struggle with my boldness, so if I could just stand next to you, that would be great. I'll walk away in a few minutes and then you can enjoy the rest of your evening."

Of course, smile as you say it, so you don't actually seem desperate, just aware of yourself.

That's what it's all about. How do you think most people would react? They might smile or give you an empathetic pat on the shoulder. Or introduce themselves. Maybe they say, "I thought I was the shyest person here. I'm glad it's you."

Think how far the conversation would go from there.

These are very personal things—your weaknesses, failings, mistakes, and hurt. But they are powerful in making a real connection.

THE POWER OF HONESTY AND CANDOR

As you increase your boldness, you will find that you can finally be honest and candid with people. That is a gift. We tell ourselves we hesitate to be honest because we don't want to hurt people, but mostly it's because we don't want them to not like or love us. But we hurt them more with dishonesty and lack of candor when it is needed most.

I know you probably don't believe that honesty is always the best policy. We certainly all have the right to have private lives and personal secrets. But be careful how closely you guard them. Be even more vigilant about telling yourself stories that the other person is better off not knowing, when it's you believing that you are better off not having the truth known.

Boldness will cure this. You will be able to speak your mind, and more importantly your heart, when it really matters, no matter how painful it may seem.

If the person doesn't respond positively to your honesty (after giving a little buffer time to let the truth be absorbed), then does that person really love *you* or just the person you're pretending to be? If it's the latter, how long can that relationship last? You're better off risking the honesty and discovering if you are accepted for your flaws and failings, and loved despite or even because of them.

Honesty isn't just a gift you give to your significant other. Yes, it builds trust and keeps everything real. But it also is a gift you give yourself. You relieve yourself of the stress of hiding something, keeping it inside, unspoken, unshared, and unaccepted. And you find out who really loves you for who you are. Plus, being honest means you don't have the stress of having to remember anything you lied about.

As Mark Twain said, "Always tell the truth. It will confound your enemies and astound your friends."

As you become more comfortable with honesty, one of the most powerful tools to integrate into communication is *candor*.

Candor is the next level of the truth. It means you are no longer disguising what you mean, making it difficult or even impossible to be accurately understood. The more candid you are, the freer you will be.

And the more effective and successful you will be. Ask any successful person if being evasive or reticent was useful to them. Bold people are straightforward, clear about their goals and intentions, and enthusiastic about getting there; they're very comfortable expressing exactly what they want from you and out of life.

Being candid also saves a significant amount of time and energy because you don't have to overthink what you want to say. It does take a certain amount of skill to speak candidly, but the more you do it, the more effective you will be at not overloading your candor with any more emotion than the situation calls for.

This is an important distinction. Don't confuse candor with unleashing your emotions without thinking. It's just the opposite. I'll give you two examples.

"You're always so mean to people!" versus, "It makes me uncomfortable when I hear what sounds like you talking down to the waitress."

Do you see the difference? The first is barfing, exaggerating your feelings and generalizing about the other person. The second is thoughtfully and calmly expressing how you feel about the immediate situation. Candor is most valuable when the speaker owns their emotion. In this example, you are not even saying that the person is indeed talking down to the waitress, but rather that to you it *sounds* like they are, and it makes you uncomfortable.

The first example here is basically character assassination, an *ad hominem* attack. It's criticism in the form of a sweeping generalization that couldn't possibly be true, and therefore it's not honest or candid but overcharged with emotion and hyperbole. It's also not likely to persuade someone to behave differently.

The art of candor involves pausing and thinking what is actually true, and then saying that. It opens an issue for discussion rather than slamming it shut. It's both accurate and honest.

One of the huge benefits of boldness is you will stop holding things in until they build up so much pressure that you have a lot of trouble being accurate and balanced. You will say things much closer to the time when you are feeling them, while also considering the Dosage that the person can handle. (The PRIDE Method shows up again!) Which means controlling your volume and intensity, and the environment where you express your candor.

You will communicate without hauling in a load of extra baggage and will therefore be understood. The true goal of candor is to be understood and to affect a possible change. Emotionally charged criticism is more about the release of negativity. Its result is seldom productive.

By the way, the worst approach is to say, "Can I be perfectly candid with you?" and when they say yes, you use it as permission to criticize without owning the emotion. Ever done that? I know you have.

Candor is positive because its intention is to achieve something positive. And I'll repeat, candor requires owning the emotion that you're feeling. It's not about expressing blame or making accusations. The best test of the honesty of your candor and your owning of the emotion? The other person actually listens.

CHAPTER 20

TIME FOR SOME
BOLD MOVES

You're ready. You've done the Boldness Exercises and integrated them into your beliefs about yourself. Now it's time for you to make connections and take actions that will matter to you. This is what you have been preparing for. Unlike the exercises, which deliberately had no intended result except to build your boldness muscle, now you are looking for real results.

Here is where you make the dismantling of your reticence, the sharpening of your social skills, and your inner relaxed state all pay off. Because now the outcome is important.

Now it's time to face your real-world stretch goals, aspirations, and wild dreams. You should have some of them in the Dream Life List of your journal already, and now is a good time to add to that list and keep adding to it for the rest of your life. Some of them are simple, singular challenges, to give your boldness wings, so to speak. Others are life-changing pursuits relating to work, relationships, or adventure.

You will return to the PRIDE Method still, but in many cases the first step, Preparation, has already happened because of the Boldness Exercises, and some of the other steps should start to become second nature as well. And, of course, Every Day Action is more important than ever. You want to use your superpower every day to make sure your brain remembers that you are bold, now and forever.

As an example, let me break down one of the most common goals, just to remind you how the PRIDE Method would be incorporated.

ASKING FOR A RAISE

This is when you are ready to test your boldness on something critical to your future. You will use the PRIDE Method with a much higher emphasis on Preparation. Here it is, PRIDE style:

Prepare: I'm going to tell you a secret about asking for a raise, based on many years of being an employer myself. The worst strategy is to explain why you need more money to pay for your lifestyle. It doesn't matter that now you have a second child or a third. Your employer won't see that as their problem. What your employer wants to know is why giving you more money makes the business more money. So, what you will prepare is an explanation of your value to the business, and how you intend to continue to improve that. You will prepare the exact words you want to say, with all the points you want to make, and then rehearse them until you own them.

Relax: You will most definitely need to relax for this one. This is 100 percent about projecting confidence, exuding from every pore that you deserve this increase, and that you could get this same amount working somewhere else. (Sounds like new words for your Daily Incantation, doesn't it? Because it should be.) Remember to BREATHE. And if you feel yourself starting to get uncomfortable, focus on your breath until it starts to calm you. Don't monologue. Anxiety will turn down your receptors, and you don't want that because you need to be listening and asking questions, which you should have prepared. Pick a good theme song to play in your head as you enter the room.

Insight: Your boss will respect you for asking for a raise, if you are properly prepared and present a good argument for how you will bring greater value to the company, even if you don't end up getting the increase. It lays the groundwork in your superior's mind that you want to earn more and are willing to do what it takes to be worthy of it. Be realistic and research the marketplace for similar jobs. In fact, if you get turned down, don't just stop there. Ask what your boss would expect from you in order for you to receive greater compensation. And listen closely.

Dosage: Dosage has a twist to it in this specific situation. Here it is more an issue of timing, getting your boss at the right moment and making sure sufficient time is allotted. Calendar it properly and leave enough time so your boss will not be distracted or rushed. You're controlling the Dosage of the experience for your boss, but also making sure you don't feel a time constraint.

Every Day Action: Guess what? Don't ask every day. Your Every Day Action in this case is bringing value. The important groundwork for asking for a raise is about two things: making your contribution significant and making your superiors aware of your contribution. People who aren't bold tend not to do anything resembling self-promotion, but the fact is that your boss cannot keep track of everything going on in her business, so she listens to the louder voices. Not that she is so naive as to fall for butt-kissing or over-confidence. But, like all of us, she remembers what has been brought to her attention.

Do you see how you modify your use of the PRIDE Method to conform to a specific bold action? You will become more skillful at this as time goes on, to the point where it's second nature. The Boldness Exercises will have prepared you, so you'll be relaxed and excited at the same time. Your Insight about bold situations will be embedded in your thinking, and you'll measure the Dosage appropriateness based on the situation, knowing that the Dosage control may not be for you but for the other person. And you'll be taking bold action every day.

One day you'll wake up and just act boldly, naturally and consistently. Because it will be you. The superpowered you. Superbold. To the world, charismatic.

Use your superpower. I'm hoping your list is already abundant with both big and small goals, but here are some suggestions, in case you need to jump-start your dream machine:

- Approaching someone you want to date
- Starting a business
- Quitting your job
- Joining a band
- Finding a mentor
- Deepening your intimacy with your mate
- Raising money for a charity you believe in by finding a major donor
- Traveling to some unfamiliar place
- Joining a club, or a team, or an association
- Mending an old friendship or family relationship
- Inviting your mate to go to therapy together to heal your relationship
- Joining a chess club, ski club, or church choir
- Spending a week in a foreign country alone
- Bungee jumping, skydiving, or hang gliding
- Going back to college
- Learning to surf, water ski, or juggle
- Attempting stand-up comedy

- Getting your motorcycle driver's license
- Joining a dance class

The list is endless, and it should be, because you are not going to die shy. You are going to be living boldly to your very last day, I hope.

Journal Entry #14: My Personal Rules

Now that you're superbold, it's time to make some commitments to yourself and establish your personal rule book. Ask yourself, "What will I do from now on, consistently, without exception? And what will I *not* do?" List these in your journal. They could be simple, like always smile and learn people's names. Or they could be big items, like always apologize, and do it quickly and sincerely. They are the ironclad, nonnegotiable parts of the you that you have become.

These are your rules. I can't write them for you. They are driven by your values and your boldness. Add to them and revise them throughout your life.

Go to your journal and make a list of all the things you will do, and all the things you won't do, ever again.

CHAPTER 21

WHY I REALLY WROTE THIS BOOK

I gave you a clue earlier about why I really wrote this book. I want you to be the person who acts, who steps up, who leans ten degrees forward, and discovers the hidden gifts that only come to the bold. Someone who realizes that they have a greater ability to have an impact, to contribute more, and improve the world around them and the lives of the people they come into contact with. I want this because this world needs bold people more than ever.

Our lives, our countries, and our planet all need people willing to take bold action and make a difference. Our problems are big and getting bigger, and it's going to take some amazing individuals to bring about the changes necessary.

Be aware that you are never done in your path to boldness. I discovered the superpower of boldness many years ago, and I'm expanding mine every day. I have much further to go. But I'm much further than I ever dreamed I would get thirty years ago. I've had amazing experiences, met extraordinary people, and enjoyed a life that has already been so fulfilling that if I died tomorrow, I would be OK. (I plan to live to at least 150, but that's for another book!)

I've stepped up in situations where it was important, and I've taken risks that have made an enormous difference in my life. I love more deeply and openly than I was ever capable of before.

Lifelong learning is essential in modern life, and, I believe, in the pursuit of true fulfillment. You will have profound achievements, wonderful memories, and glorious moments along the way. But it is always a journey. You may be graduating to the next level, but you'll never be out of school.

You may need to be bold enough to demand a promotion. You may need to ask your spouse for a divorce. You may need to ask your father for an apology for his violence. Whatever you might need to speak up about, you will not want to be silent anymore.

The love of your life is waiting out there. Or your future business partner. Or a new good friend. Or a better job. Or just a brief, lovely, pleasant, or inspiring interaction with a complete stranger. Maybe someone's life will need to be saved. Or someone will be in a desperate state, and you will be the one who steps up. You are no longer the bystander in any situation.

Seize the day, every day.

What I hope will happen, and I believe will happen for many of you, is your dreams will expand, and your goals will become larger, because you tolerate risk and failure gleefully, and you're not governed by fear and loss, or embarrassment or negativity.

As I said, more than ever, we need people who are willing to step up and change the world. That could easily be you by simply making the decision to be that person. All it requires is the boldness to believe you could reach that goal, to have a vision for your life as someone who can make a real difference in hundreds of people's lives, or thousands, or millions. It's all up to you.

What I've observed over more than sixty years is only the bold individuals change the world, those who are undaunted by other people's judgments and daring enough to chase the highest ideals and the biggest dreams. You know their names: Abraham Lincoln, Amelia Earhart, Walt Disney, Bill Gates, Mother Teresa, Mahatma Gandhi, Martin Luther King Jr., Steve Jobs, Meryl Streep, Elon Musk. Nothing prevents you from adding your name to that list.

Increasing your potential, elevating your capabilities, and expanding your impact on the world will be where the true meaning comes in your life. It will only stop when your heart does. So, show up and present the real, best you to the world every day. The new and improved one, that is just a little bit better than yesterday.

Because no matter what, for you, there's no going back. You're bold now. Enjoy your superpower.

YOUR BOLDNESS JOURNAL

This book is about taking action. An essential part of that will be logging your results on a daily basis, so a journal is critical. I recommend making it a physical journal, with a nice cover on it, because this is your transformation manual, and you want it to be tangible. I do believe there is something about having a real object, like a talisman symbolizing and empowering your growth and transformation. Trust me on this.

And keep it private. This is for your eyes only.

If you absolutely must go digital, then use an app like Evernote so that you are putting everything in the right place and can access it anywhere on any device.

Also, you will have the opportunity to do testimonial posts on my website, where you can talk about your greatest successes and failures, and exercises that you created yourself. It will be a great experience for you to share your evolution and see what other people have experienced.

Your Boldness Journal has three purposes: to track your progress, both the failures and the victories; to reflect on your past, for motivation to become even bolder; and to lay out your dreams and goals. The more dedicated you are to detailing these thoughts and experiences, the faster you will progress in confidence, boldness, and fulfillment. Re-read them often for inspiration and guidance.

JOURNAL SECTIONS

I recommend you copy the directions for each section into your journal so you'll have them for reference.

#1. Moments That Made a Difference

List any moment, or action, where you took bold action and it changed the course of your life. Think back and list all the times when you did or said exactly what you wanted to. What happened? How did it feel? When did speaking up make a difference? When did you get more than you expected because you acted? Also, list what situations you already act with confidence in, either because you are highly skilled or just naturally feel comfortable.

#2. My Missed Opportunities

List anytime when you hesitated and the moment passed, when you could have met someone, introduced yourself, said something good, or been helpful or encouraging, or took a big risk. Write them here whenever you recall another one. Then also add:

- What did you miss out on?
- What could you have said or done?
- What difference would that have made in your life?

Highlight when someone gave you a golden opportunity, laid it right out in front of you, and you still missed it. These get a special label all their own, called "Super Goofs."

#3. My Barrier Beliefs

What are the beliefs you hold, your negative self-programming, the messages from Doctor No, that you've used to define yourself? List them now and add to them every time you catch yourself thinking another one. Every time you hear your inner voice playing a discouraging thing, or a barrier belief, or an excuse why you won't attempt something, write it down. Then make a note if you think it's really true. You may likely come back later and see if it's still true ninety days from now. If not, make a notation of how you've overwritten this code to define yourself better.

#4. My Crutches

What are the excuses you give yourself for why you are not acting boldly? What are the crutches you fall back on, however large or trivial, true or fantasy?

#5. Ranking Other People's Opinions

List all the people that you are close to in life, in work, family, and fun. Then, on a scale of 1 to 10, lay out how much each person's opinion about you should matter (you can put in your own score—these are mine):

Your spouse/partner: 8 (It should matter almost as much as yours, but not replace it.)

Mentors: 9 (If your mentor's opinion doesn't matter almost as much as your own, why are they your mentor?)

Close friends: 10

Facebook "friends": 1

Coworkers: 4

Audience members: 5

Random strangers' opinions: 0

Exercise Results

You are now doing the Boldness Exercises, and you will want to be recording what happened with each of them here in your journal.

For each exercise, record these details:

- Date and time
- What did you say or do?
- What was the reaction of the other person? What happened?
- How did you feel before?
- How did you feel after?
- What worked?
- What PRIDE steps did you miss?
- What could you have said or done instead?
- What more could you have said or done to continue the encounter beyond the exercise?
- Was it a success? Or a lesson? (You win either way!)
- How many attempts did it take to act or speak?
- Celebrate! Reward yourself for your bold move!

#6. My Fantasy Encounter List

List anyone you would like to meet, no matter how unlikely it would be.

Here is a suggested list of living people that it may seem incredibly unlikely that you would ever meet, but it would be very exciting to you if you did:

- Sir Richard Branson
- Bill Clinton
- George W. Bush
- Bradley Cooper
- Meryl Streep
- Ellen DeGeneres
- Kamala Harris
- Lady Gaga
- Mark Zuckerberg
- Bill Gates
- Elon Musk

Get the idea?

#7. My Realistic Encounters List

What person or people would you really like to meet that you could meet in the next week or two if you were just bold enough?

Some suggestions:

- Your CEO
- That guy in the finance department
- That gal in marketing
- That singer in the club you like
- A multimillionaire entrepreneur
- The appealing person you see in the grocery store every week
- Your favorite author

#8. My Dream Life List

Who do you want to become? What do you want to achieve? What's on your bucket list? For the moment, let go of how long it might take or how much money would be required. These can be fanciful, be a one-time thing, or take a lifetime, but stay in the range of what's possible. They can be deeply personal as well. Here are some suggestions:

- Get a ride to the International Space Station
- Get knighted by the Queen of England
- Jump onstage and sing backup to Lady Gaga
- Meet a life partner
- Become a CEO
- Create a charitable foundation
- Live in Europe for a month
- Skydive
- Learn salsa dancing
- Swim with sharks
- Open a restaurant
- Heal my relationship with my father

#9. Incantations

What are you going to tell yourself every day, as if it's already true? List all the incantations you create over time and notice the progression. You should also be adding them as sticky notes on your mirror.

#10. My Cringeworthy Moments

These are the events or encounters in your past where you:

- Spoke up or acted, but did it so awkwardly that the result was painfully bad or embarrassing.
- Said or did the wrong thing, but never apologized or explained yourself later.
- The painful moments that haunt you, for one reason or another.
- What scared you?

With each one, also write what you could have said or done differently. Also list what you believe you missed out on.

#11. Meanings I Could Change

Take a few moments and think of two or three experiences that really bothered or hurt you and probably still do. They could be very significant in your life or only mildly so. Write them down and then come up with at least two alternative meanings.

Start with the fact, and then your interpretation, and then add the meanings.

#12. Positive Judgments

Write down every judgment you have about anyone for an entire day, both the negative and then the positive one you replaced it with. Repeat this each week for a month, and then once every month for a year. You might want to use a separate notepad for this, or the Evernote app on your phone.

#13. Defusing Cringeworthy Moments

Find the person with whom the cringeworthy event, or the moment, or the exchange occurred. Apologize, if necessary, and explain it. If you can't find the person, tell a friend. Make an entry on these three things:

1. How did it feel to express it?
2. What was the reaction to the apology and explanation?
3. Did you feel released from the cringe-worthiness?
   (I sure hope so!)

#14. My Personal Rules

What will you do or not do from now on?

This is where you will start to list the things that you will do consistently, without exception. You will add to this list as you become more comfortable doing more things. They are ironclad, nonnegotiable. Make your own list with your own rules. Use my suggestions if you need to, but they need to be rules you intend to follow.

For example:

1. Always ask a person's name. And remember it. Even if I have to ask three more times.
2. Always start on a positive note with anyone I meet.
3. Apologize quickly and sincerely.
4. Never go to sleep without having made at least one person feel good about themselves.
5. Never let a day pass without venturing out of my comfort zone.
6. Always be considerate, knowing that I may still make some people uncomfortable.
7. Use my superpower for good, not just for myself, but for others.
8. Dream bigger.

ANNUAL REVIEW

At least annually, reread these entries. See how much you've changed. And have that precious insight that you are still you, just a much better version. For PDFs of the journal and the Boldness Exercises, go to www. fredjoyal.com/superbold.

ACKNOWLEDGMENTS

Some of these individuals contributed to my path to superboldness and others contributed to the creation of this book. I am grateful to them all.

I realize this is the part of a book that most people don't read, so I'll try to be brief and interesting.

To Norman Blier, who gave me my first job. May he rest in peace, as he was not a peaceful man when he was alive.

To Ron Margolin, my friend and professor at the University of Rhode Island. He was my first true mentor and ground a lot of the rough edges off me. I appreciate him tolerating my ignorance about almost everything.

To Ken Berris, who gave me my first job as an advertising copywriter. My boldness began to blossom in that creative environment, and I'm deeply grateful for him believing in me.

To Gary Saint Denis, my business partner. We made a big, bold move together, and it paid off. I treasure our enduring friendship.

To all my teachers at the Groundlings Improv School in Los Angeles. You made me laugh, and you made me a whole lot bolder.

To Ruben Paul, who insisted I try stand-up comedy, knowing I had the deep-seated desire to do it. You were my comedy shepherd, and I'll always be grateful.

To Dr. Mark Morin, who was the first one to ever give me stage time.

And who also taught me how to stay up all night and still deliver a great lecture the next morning.

To Kaleim and Rezwan Manji, who brought me into their Young & Motivated program when we were all a lot younger. It lit the spark that led me to this book.

To Christine Price, who taught me how to express my emotions, as she did for countless others. There will always be a special place in my heart for you, Chris.

To Dr. Bill Dorfman, who inspires me with all his bold endeavors, and also for giving me a chance to do my boldness lecture in front of his LEAP group. It was the final boost I needed to get this book done.

To Tony Robbins, whose phenomenal messages I successfully resisted for twenty years. I'm glad I finally listened.

To Tim Ferriss. You "opened your kimono" and taught me and many others that weekend how to get a book done.

To Bernie Stoltz and all the team at Fortune Management. You inspire me and challenge me, but most of all, you are precious friends.

To everyone at Scribe Media, especially my extraordinary editor, Tashan Mehta. Tucker Max, they do you proud.

To everyone who encouraged me over the years, thank you. It empowered me.

To everyone who rejected me over the years, thank you. It strengthened me.

And finally, to you, dear reader, for reading all the way through the acknowledgments. May you rise up and make the world a better place and be the voice of upliftment wherever you go.

ABOUT THE AUTHOR

FRED JOYAL is an author, speaker, entrepreneur, and business advisor. Along with a lucrative career in advertising and marketing, he co-founded the most successful dentist referral service in the country, 1-800-DENTIST. He has written two books on marketing, dabbled in stand-up and improv comedy, acted in bad movies and excellent TV commercials, and visited over forty-four countries around the world. He has an honorary Doctor of Arts degree from the University of Rhode Island, perhaps because of his generous donations. He once beat Sir Richard Branson in chess and was also an answer on *Jeopardy!*. He is an avid cyclist, a below-average tennis player, and an even worse golfer.

He can be reached at fred@fredjoyal.com, and more information and resources are available at fredjoyal.com.

CPSIA information can be obtained
at www.ICGtesting.com
Printed in the USA
LVHW090831091121
702655LV00027B/495/J